'It doesn't matter how rich or poor a person is, what gender or social class, or how much fame or education she possesses; verbal, mental, and physical abuse can happen to anyone. It doesn't matter what a woman's ethnicity is because the only distinguishing colour of abuse is black-and-blue.'

La Toya Jackson

'So, having regard to my impressions of both of them, whilst it is physical abuse, not of the worst kind it has to be said, this is a physical manifestation of the father ensuring that his point of view had to be made and was being made forcibly to the mother.'

'So, whilst I find that the father was unable to control himself or his temper and is guilty of aggressive and controlling and coercive conduct at the time of the separation, I do not find that his behaviour was such as to found the very serious position which the mother now appears to find herself.....'

UK High Court Judge, Family Division, 2021, Parental Alienation decision against the mother in fact finding hearing

In June 2020, the Ministry of Justice published the final report of its expert panel on assessing risk of harm to children and parents in private family law children cases. The report, referred to as the 'Harm Report' noted that the family courts do not effectively protect many child and adult victims of domestic abuse from further harm.

The pro-contact culture of the courts and professionals involved in child arrangement cases; submissions highlighted a resulting lack of understanding of the different forms that domestic abuse takes, of the ongoing impacts of abuse on children and victim parents, the systematic minimisation or disbelief of abuse, and the acceptance of counter allegations without robust scrutiny.

Until recently there has been very limited understanding in the legal system about coercive control as a component of domestic abuse. The criminal justice system, in particular, has been heavily focused on single incidents of physical violence and not responsive to other forms of abuse.

However, the reality of domestic abuse for many victims is the micro management of their lives in multiple ways, which leaves them in a state of constant fear and anxiety.

Assessing Risk of Harm to Children and Parents in Private Law Children Cases (Harm Report) UK Ministry of Justice, June 2020[1]

'Despite finding some good practice and well-intentioned staff, the Panel exposed deep-seated systemic failings which, in the worst cases, put victims of domestic abuse and their children at risk. The Panel found that too often, adversarial court proceedings retraumatised victims. Allegations of domestic abuse were too readily disbelieved or dismissed, alongside poor risk assessments and siloed working... .'

Assessing Risk of Harm to Children and Parents in Private Law Children Cases – Implementation Plan: delivery update UK Ministry of Justice, May 2023[2]

'Domestic violence is one of the most serious and pervasive human rights violations, in particular as it affects women and girls. While men can also fall victims to domestic violence, women are at a much higher risk and the dynamics of abuse are different for men.

As noted in a number of submissions, domestic violence and parental alienation are often blurred in family law systems, to the detriment of the victims of violence…'

UN Report on Custody, violence against women and violence against children Report of the Special Rapporteur on violence against women and girls, its causes and consequences, April 2023[3]

PRINCE CHARMING

A journey of escaping domestic abuse through pain, fear, helplessness, darkness and isolation to hope, survival and freedom and insights to navigate the UK family justice system.

Sophia Chiose

WMP

Prince cHarming

Sophia Chiose

First published in September 2023

WM Publishing

ISBN 978-1-914265-82-2 ebk

ISBN 978-1-914265-83-9 pbk

A CIP catalogue record for this book is available from the British Library.

CONTENTS

Please Read This First

When you steal something, in most countries this is seen as a crime and punishment will be metered out with attempts to deter and stop future attempts to steal – but why is it OK for a man to steal from a woman and this be ignored because it happens in a relationship or domestic setting? Why is it OK for a man to steal a woman's confidence, her identity, her self- worth, her dignity, her independence, her choices, her safety, her freedom?

This book is about the journey of those women who have or are still escaping domestic abuse, not just from their partner, but from the family justice system itself. This book provides insights into the experience of women at the hands of their partners, courts, judges, lawyers and a myriad of professionals that do not truly see or truly hear or understand these women or their experiences and provides some supporting information to help navigate it.

While this is a true account of the author's personal journey, she is using a pen name to protect the identity of her children; and has deliberately made superficial changes to the story to comply with the Court rulings. But she has not altered or embellished the facts. **In any case, any similarity to actual persons, living or dead, or actual events, is purely coincidental.**

This is a journey through pain, fear, helplessness, darkness and isolation to hope, survival and freedom.

The author does not wish to focus on her ethnicity, her age or social, religious, cultural, educational background- because domestic abuse does not discriminate, and unfortunately, her story, may one day become another woman's.

This journey is being shared to help other women to understand the process of abuse, process of finally escaping the abuse, the challenges along the way, experiences of the family justice system (which is a reference to courts, judges, police, social workers, family therapists, lawyers and other professionals involved in the family justice system in the UK) and information to help regain some control or at least understanding but mostly to let women know that someone understands what they are truly experiencing and believes them and that they are not alone, even in the isolation of domestic abuse.

Foreword

Navigating the hell of domestic abuse is like trying to escape quicksand from the bottom of a hole; each time you try to cling onto something to get out, you get thrown back in. Some days you get tired of doing simple things like trying to stand up; other days you want to die because it seems easier; and some (rare) times you feel brave enough to want to escape. Mostly, however, you live in fear, walk on eggshells, or you simply feel broken, numb, violated, exploited and empty. You may be beaten, hit, kicked, screamed at, emotionally abused, financially controlled, undermined, spat at, subjected to coercive and controlling behaviour, slapped, or locked in rooms and more…

With some or all of this somehow becoming your normality, let me tell you what I wish someone had told me: even if any culture, tradition, religion, system or patriarchy tells you that any of the above is OK, or normal, or just happens in relationships sometimes, it is NOT OK and apparently even against the law[4,5] … Would you think it is OK for a total stranger to be treated in the same way?

So, when – or if – you find the courage, strength, or do or die trigger to manage an escape, you may end up in one or many courts. At which point, navigating away from your abuser is like being thrown on a chess board and forced to participate in a game whilst being blindfolded with no instructions. A myriad of other parties will join your journey, positioning you (and your children) as pawns. Every effort will be made to set you up to lose, especially when children are involved, or if you are a woman who is perceived to be strong or does not appear in the stereotypical image of an abused woman (blood and bruises being the optimal look!).[6]

The 'game' may start with your 'loved one' who started the abuse, but others may join his team and surround you. His teammates might include friends and extended family, often being the first point of minimising the abuse or sanctioning it (accentuated by culture and social norms in some cases), as well as the courts, social workers and family therapists and more. Some will also be waiting to financially exploit your vulnerability.

The family justice system, unfortunately, may be a place where the abuse is further enabled, making you wonder if staying in the abuse was better than the perpetual hell you find yourself in when trying to escape from the abuser… and that treadmill that never stops. If you make it into the family justice system, you will face numerous people who have NEVER lived your experiences; people who have little or no empathy towards you; all who make decisions for you and your children – including purported specialists[7,8] or therapists and other participants in the process. All of whom will make significant financial gain, even if their reports or recommendations may be considered unhelpful or may lead to traumatic experiences for mothers and children'[9,10]. Professionals that should be supporting all family members, such as social workers, may exercise discretion to omit facts while making notes and records in your matter, sending sick children to contact, denying facts that they have previously put in writing, or ignoring legal communications; and so on.

Engagement with these people may make you question your own reality, make you doubt your own mind, put you under optimal pressure to make you break down through constant attack and criticism whilst you stand alone – blindfolded – unable to see that your life is being treated as a game.

Understanding what you may be subjected to may help you to understand what you can also learn to overcome.

Breaking The Abuse Cycle

Abuse requires control and fear: control over your mind, and instilling fear. Unfortunately, the family justice system may also instil fear in mothers; that they will lose their children in cases where domestic abuse is alleged which will commonly be countered with accusations of parental alienation to minimise or dismiss the abuse, even if this has traumatic consequences for the mother.[7] This 'gagging' of mothers through fear allows the abuse to continue.[1,3,8] But knowledge is power and with knowledge you may be able to reclaim at least some degree of control over your mind and over your reactions to what may be thrown at you.

My name is Sophia Chiose (not my real name, as I will explain). That said, this is my account of my journey and insights which I gathered through the process; something I wish someone had warned me about before I set out on making my escape.

My journey is still not over, nor has it been made easy, but with research, knowledge and awareness, navigating the endless biased process is at least becoming more familiar.

Even as I write this, the independent social workers allocated to my matter contacted me while in recovery from the removal of a tumour, even though they had, a few days before, been legally requested not to have siloed discussions with the father to the exclusion of my children and I. They continued to ignore this. I am now past disbelief as to what will continue to happen, but not defeated, unfortunately other women have lost all hope, died or even killed themselves[11] and so I wanted to share with you the message of hope, because that is the light that I held onto that carried me and still carries me out of this darkness.

Hopefully you can find some support and insight in these pages, none of which is legal or financial advice, nor any form of counselling, but may hopefully help you navigate whatever stage of abuse you are going through, even those of you who may not yet have recognised you are being abused.

> 'One of the first barriers to raising domestic abuse is that the victim of the abuse must themselves appreciate that they have experienced abuse. Often it takes victims of nonphysical abuse a long time to acknowledge that they have experienced abuse. Once abuse is recognised by the victim, it is very helpful for them not to feel alone when they are trying to raise that abuse with children's social care, Cafcass/Cymru and the court.
>
> The fear of disbelief is a significant factor dissuading victims from raising allegations. ......'[12]
>
> *UK Ministry of Justice 'Harm Report', June 2020.*

Light At The End Of The Tunnel?

The black hole or tunnel we find ourselves in may feel endless, indeed the opening segments from the family justice system may feel that domestic abuse is a never-ending horror, or simply does not exist other than in the victim's mind or narrative. But this book may serve as a torch of hope to guide you through the darkness of domestic abuse and to let you know that someone can hear you, understand you and believe you.

'Victims and survivors must rely on the Family Court to keep their children safe from perpetrators. Yet too often victims and survivors do not feel understood or taken seriously in the Family Court. In turn, this undermines the sense of faith held by the public in the family justice system, which often places victims and survivors at further risk'.

The Domestic Abuse Commissioner's second report on the Family Court and domestic abuse. Presented to Parliament pursuant to section 8(6) of the Domestic Abuse Act 2021. July 2023

"The secrecy around the Family Court creates a lot of trauma. Women go into the process thinking that they are going to get justice and their abuse will be acknowledged, but that is not what the Family Court can offer."

Victim/survivor of domestic abuse who attended the Domestic Abuse Commissioner's roundtable discussion on the Family Court (September 2021).

The system may feel broken, but you can learn to navigate this 'broken' system without it breaking you.[13,14]

I promise.

Part 1

My Story: Going In

1

August Ten Years Ago

'WHAT DID YOU FUCKING SAY?!' my 'loving' husband yells while chasing me up the stairs in his sister's house.

I run into the bedroom we are staying in. I am scrambling to shut the door. I can't lock it quickly enough while protecting our six-week-old baby sleeping in a sling on my chest. While I am fumbling to lock the door, he bursts the door open and continues with a barrage of swearing. He foams at the mouth f'ing and blinding.

I'm clutching my baby with all my love, retreating and withdrawing and using my arms as a shield over my baby and my face. Walking backwards with arms shielded over both of us, I eventually hit the wardrobes behind me. I have nowhere to go. He shouts into my ear; his hot breath burning my ear lobes spitting at me as his words get louder and louder near my face.

I close my eyes. Seconds feel like hours.

Someone pulls at my arms. I pull my daughter and shielding arms closer to my chest, not knowing who is trying to tug my arms away from my baby girl.

'It's me, give me the baby.'

His sister's voice is little relief – relief, nonetheless. I loosen the sling and hand the baby to her whilst her husband holds Prince Harming back from me and tries to usher him downstairs while still ranting about how disgusting I am, and disgusting my family is and I have no respect... his ranting continues on and on as he is carefully ushered out of the room to stop him directing his anger back at me.

I close the door and stand in silence facing the ground.

I am broken.

I feel embarrassed, engulfed by shame

Welcome to a 'normal' day in my life......

2

Meeting Prince cHarming

So, how does this story begin?

True to any fairy tale girls are introduced to from the time they can read; the vision of Prince Charming is someone who will 'save you' and fill your life with happiness – complete you – for without him you are incapable of all happy things, unable to make decisions, and unable to understand what is best for you. This indoctrination across cultures, races and countries unfortunately causes girls to disbelieve their own power, or worse – believe they have none.

When I was very young and impressionable, I was raised in a culture and tradition where independent decision-making by a female was not the norm. Cultural patriarchy and social norms dominated expected behaviour. Most aspects of the real world were shielded from me, perhaps to protect me or maybe to comply with societal expectations of how girls should and should not behave. This buffering from the world resulted in disabling me from being able to navigate the realities of the world when I finally ventured out on my own in young adulthood, nor being able to set my own boundaries or recognise that I was enduring abuse.

Cultural entrenchment having unintended consequences of disabling and disempowering women.

Whilst I grew up, witnessing domestic abuse and cultural restraints, with my mother taking out her frustrations on myself and my siblings, it was the norm for men to 'do' and women to conform. Growing up was done with societal approval at the forefront of our minds, with clear expectation of how girls and women were expected to behave. I grew up with pressure to overachieve and outperform in order to compete for attention and seek approval.

Fortunately, however, with my dad's blessing, being his favourite, I was the first girl in our family to attend university. This, fortuitously (perhaps to my detriment), delayed any opportunity of an 'arranged' marriage.

And this is where I met Prince Charming.

University - Twenty Five Years Ago

Leaving home for the first time was refreshing.

I was studying law in London, living in halls and soon making lots of friends through one of the university social groups. I found like-minded people in what was still a racist society in East London at the time. That was a comfort. One of those friends was a British-Asian (sub-continent) man I refer to on these pages as Prince Charming – who first grabbed my attention when I saw him appear late to a lecture. Making his grand entrance, he was tall and handsome.

A friend properly introduced us when I was in the library one day. From that day on, he was charming, meeting me in the library whenever I went and always studying alongside me. Conversations flowed freely. Whilst we spoke different dialects, and Prince Charming had a different religion and upbringing, we ate the same food and had a lot in common. He charmed me with doughnuts he bought from my favourite shop – the express way to my nineteen-year-old heart. He was attentive, kind and shy – often visiting me in my halls of residence to bring me gifts. If I wasn't in my room when he was looking for me, he tracked me down through friends, which I thought was sweet; I hadn't ever had anyone chase after me like that before and previously had to work extremely hard to get any recognition.

3

Forbidden Love

Our friendship became quite intense during the first year of university, especially after a university trip to Wales but I knew I couldn't tell anyone about him because an inter-religious relationship with a Muslim man was taboo.

Prince Charming and eight university friends planned the trip to Wales. Prince Charming had contacts in Wales, so we had all our food and tour arrangements prepared for us for the trip.

One day, we decided we would like to go for a drive in the Welsh countryside but everybody aside from Prince Charming pulled out at the last minute – as if planned by our friends. Still, Prince Charming and I went out together. It was terribly eerie out there, but he kept me calm by talking about the environment and the planet – all subjects I enjoyed.

Only, we were trying to navigate a small country lane on the way home when we got stuck in a ditch. Stranded in the middle of the Welsh countryside, he held my hand and comforted me while we waited for a tow vehicle. It was then that I knew I felt safe with him (or thought I was safe).

When help came, Prince Charming sat with me during our drive home, and I knew we were an item. Little did I know that we would keep our relationship entirely secret from both of our families for several years.

Two Years Later

I graduated with a 2:1 in law through wanting to overachieve and decided to continue studying to avoid entering an arranged marriage. I went to law school and then read a Masters – eventually graduating with a Merit.

Academically, I was excelling.

At this time, Prince Charming had gone to law school to train as a solicitor, but we were together and life was good.

Three Years Later

I had bought an apartment and started putting down roots for my future, also starting a new job in the City of London.

Around this time, I began to notice that Prince Charming was quite domineering, telling me that he was going to go somewhere for a weekend, for example, without discussing it with me. If I questioned him, he told me he would do whatever he wanted and that there was no debating it. Apparently, I should get used to that. He then told me that he would leave me if I didn't listen to him or do as he said. I knew no different than men *saying* and women *doing*.

It was his way or no way. That was just culture to me – to do as a man told me.

Whilst I was a little irritated by having to just put up and shut up, I was timid. I was in love. My whole world would collapse if Prince Charming left me. I was scared. I would do anything to prevent that from happening.

4

Alone – Far Far Away

January, Twenty Years Ago

One evening, Prince Charming and I were having dinner when he said, 'I like the Middle East, I think we should move there.'

I didn't know anything about the place or where his excitement had originated from.

We agreed to go on holiday there to see what it was like and had a wonderful time enjoying the glitz and glamour. I was young. And it was exciting.

When we returned to the UK, and Prince Charming reiterated that we should move to the Middle East, I started looking for jobs. A job vacancy advert appeared for a country in the Middle East that was building a new business district and looking for experienced ex-pat workers.

One week later, I was successfully interviewed by the CEO. Two weeks later I was packing up and shipping my belongings to the Middle East. There I was, in my late twenties, not knowing much about the Middle East, and packing my bags to move to a desert country to start a new job when anxiety and panic started to set in about leaving my home, my friends and family and being alone in a new country.

'I don't want to go,' I told Prince Charming.

'You have to.'

'I really am not sure about this.'

'You must go.'

His decision was made, and I did what he said.

I didn't even know why he was so keen to move to the Middle East – and we certainly were not going to discuss his reasons – but for the fact his larger-than-life personality suited it.

So, off I went.

New Beginnings?

Prince Charming and I left the UK together to drop me to the Middle East to start my new role, before he returned to the UK and continue applying for jobs in the Middle East.

My employers housed me in a hotel apartment for one month until I found permanent accommodation, so everything was arranged for the beginning a new life. Co-habiting outside of marriage was forbidden.

On the third day, I was left alone and sat in my air-conditioned hotel apartment wondering what the hell I was doing there. I did not like the initial move and was very homesick for the first six months, often telephoning Prince Charming to tell him I wanted to return to the UK.

'We've decided this together. You are going to stay there. End of conversation.'

So I persevered.

5

Blinded by Love

Autumn Twenty Years Ago

Prince Charming was still looking for jobs whilst I remained alone in the Middle East. My employers were beginning to get worried about me because, although I was doing well at work, it was clear that I wasn't putting down roots. My colleagues had rented their own homes, bought a car, and ingrained themselves in Middle Eastern society. I had not.

And I felt as though I was in limbo.

When I told my employers that the problem was that we couldn't find Prince Charming any work, they found him a job and he finally moved over that December.

When he went to start his job at a prominent law firm, nobody showed up to greet him. He came to my house and took it out on me.

'You made me leave my job in London and nobody turned up. *This is your fault!*'

I was upset that he was unhappy and blamed myself for not having everything properly organised for him, but I look back now and realise that this was not my doing.

This was actually the second time I had helped him get a job. This job, later on, turned out to give him access to the most prominent deals and people in the Middle East.

Either way, I didn't control the law firm he was starting work for – but I was besotted and thought my world would collapse around me if he was no longer beside me. I took the blame – for everything – as he would often tell me that he would leave me if I pushed him or questioned him, and of course, told I would be nothing without him.

*

Prince Charming eventually settled into work and met lots of important people. An expat man can feel like a king in some parts of the Middle East if he wants to because there are plenty of people living the high life, with fast cars, penthouse apartments, and some of the hippest restaurants and bars in the world. Prince Charming fell for that within nine months. He was going out a lot with new friends while I was working and looking after my home.

We didn't officially live together but we spent a lot of time together.

More distance grew between us.

To my shock, he then decided he wanted space from me.

Why had I gone to set up our lives there if he didn't want to be a part of it? Moving there was all his idea, after all.

But *I was to blame for the breakdown in our relationship.*

Everything was my fault.

I was heartbroken. Confused. Angry – with myself.

I felt as though I had to continue my work at the new business district because I had left my career in London and it would be career suicide to leave my job halfway through.

Most of all, however, I wanted reconciliation, even though I didn't know what I had done to create this distance between us.

6

The Air Hostess

Eighteen Years Ago

Eight or so months passed before I found out why everything had changed. And, after all that worry, none of it was my fault like I had wondered – although I was blamed for it.

Prince Charming had been seeing an air hostess for a number of months.

Somebody told me what was going, so I gave her a call when I came across her number. 'Hello, I'm looking for Prince Charming. Is he there, please?'

'Who are you?'

'I'm his girlfriend.'

She was clearly upset when she realised there might be another girl in his life. We left the phone call at that point, but she then phoned me back a few times to try to get the truth.

Through those conversations, it transpired that Prince Charming had told the air hostess that his mum lived in an upmarket part of town, supposedly being Middle East origin. He had also told her his family were influential in the Middle East – all made up. I did not even recognise the man she was describing. I also learnt that Prince Charming and the air hostess had travelled abroad together, so his absence and need for space was all making sense.

I confronted him about it and he told me that it was all in my head – denying all liability.

*

Taking matters into my own hands, I invited Prince Charming to my house having pre-arranged for the air hostess to be there. When he arrived at my house, the air hostess wasn't yet there. She arrived and was also upset about being duped, so when he denied what was going on, she proved their relationship by revealing intimate details of their relationship.

I stood there wondering who this man was. Had everything we shared together been a lie?

Prince Charming ignored me and seemed to be more interested in snapping back at the air hostess until he lost his temper and shouted, *'Fuck you all!'*

And he reminded me that it was my fault that I was not giving him time and attention but the air hostess was – again this was all my fault.

He then left the house. I went after him to try and make some sense of what had just happened. He was leaving in a hurry, so I got halfway into his car to talk with him. He wasn't interested in speaking, so I tried to get out of the car. He accelerated – causing me to stumble out of the car (and that was not the last time he did that to me).

Prince Charming sped off into the night.

At that point, I was thinking it was all over. Finished.

I couldn't believe what he was doing to me. I had put the evidence in front of him, in **DARK BOLD**, and he *still* denied it.

It's hard to make any sense of what was happening at that time except that he believed his own lies – something that continues today.

Prince Charming was gradually becoming *Prince Harming*.

But I *still* could not see it.

7

Black Hole?

I shut down following the incident with the air hostess. Cut Prince Harming out of my life. How could I be with such a blatant liar? That chapter in my life was over. Eight years wasted. The trouble was, however, that I didn't know how to be alone because he was my first real boyfriend, with whom I had been with since I was nineteen. He had, initially, made me feel safe.

Being alone in a foreign country was a steep learning curve. I kept slogging away with my work, focussing almost all of my energies on that – doing what I did when I was a child – over-performing to prove my self-worth.

Then, flowers started arriving on my doorstep and Prince Harming tried contacting me to reconcile our relationship. I wasn't one bit interested. He persevered, like an ant, reappearing just when I thought I had gotten rid of him – using his persuasive powers to suck me back into his life.

Aged late twenties, living in the Middle East and wondering whether there was anything better for me, I started succumbing to his constant draw, a technique which I now know as 'hoovering'.

What else was there for me?

Then, he said, 'You know what, we've had these issues and I'm sorry for my part in what's occurred, but we have been together for a long time and it would be a shame to part.'

Like an idiot, I believed him.

We went out for drinks. Had dinner. He begged for forgiveness, turned on the tears – he was great at turning on the waterworks whenever he thought it might help change my mind. Just as he thought he had reeled me in, the crimson warning lights began flashing in my head. 'I can't do this. I can't do this,' I said while fighting my emotions with all that I had. But I felt myself weakening.

He pleaded some more. Cried some more. Breaking me down. One. Little. Bit. At. A. Time.

'I've forgiven you for not being there for me that caused the distance, why can't you forgive me? Free yourself, be happy with me again, remember all that we had?'

He was twisting and turning my head. I wanted to believe him.

He then invited his cousin to meet me. I remember being very shy because Prince Harming hadn't fully invited me into his family's life before. A tidal wave of emotion swept me out to sea and I sailed with it. Then, Prince Harming's cousin was told to tell Prince Harming's mother about us.

'Is there an *us*?' I was thinking... I started believing there was, so I told my sister about my relationship – who told my mum and dad. They were HORRIFIED that I had chosen a Muslim man.

'You've disgraced the family. This is not what I expected from you. You've made your bed, now lie on it,' they said.

I suddenly found myself back in a relationship, without planning to. And now that I had told Mum and Dad about it, I only had Prince Harming to confide in. My parents had basically disowned me. 'Which way do I turn now?' I asked myself.

'I think we should get married,' Prince Harming then said.

Every single warning light in my head was now flashing crimson because I knew it was a bad idea, but I let it roll and the wedding plans spiralled out of my control.

What was I doing?!

Weeks went by… Wedding plans unrolled…

'I can't do this.'

'Yes, you can.'

I went with the flow, not really understanding what I was doing. This was all unfolding barely a few months after the standoff with Prince Harming and the air hostess.

8

Marriage One

Seventeen Years Ago

Prince Harming had ostentatious plans for our wedding. We would arrange a grand civil marriage in Greece, but would first set off to meet Prince Harming's family in Coventry because his mother insisted that we should be married in the eyes of God before becoming legally married.

His mother seemed OK when I first met her. Although, she told me that I would have to convert to Islam and that any children of ours would also be Muslim.

'OK,' I said. I was now scared, and wanted to return to my familiar life, but Prince Harming had assured me that this was *only a formality* and that our lives would be the same as they always were in the Middle East.

'Just agree with what you are asked. Nothing will change, I promise.'

'Do your parents approve?' Prince Harming's mother asked.

'No.'

My mother-in-law understood that because many non-Muslim girls marrying Muslim men are disowned by their families.... and I was about to become another statistic.

With the Islamic marriage plans set for the following week, I was told how I would be converted to Islam on the day of the wedding.

*

The morning of the ceremony. I woke up feeling dread and anxiety. I wondered what I was doing, but I didn't have time to think because I was driven to Prince Harming's cousins house. There, I was introduced to the rest of the family. To be fair, they were very attentive and welcoming.

None of my family was there, however.

I look back now and wonder what I was thinking. Part of me felt like it was not real and that I was just following the motion. I was not in the present, like a disassociated, out-of-body experience – *there but not there* – but, Prince Harming had assured me this was just a formality; that our lives would not change.

The Islamic ceremony began. I was given an Islamic name- Alia. The Islamic scholar recited something that I repeated before witnesses. Five minutes later, I was married – not having even seen Prince Harming by this stage. I was then led downstairs while he was completing his part of the marriage in a separate room. With the Islamic marriage certificate signed, we were married in the eyes of God – almost mechanically.

I flew back to the Middle East alone that evening because I had to go back to work. It sounds weird because it was. Prince Harming stayed behind and seemed unphased by sending me back alone as newly 'married'.

9

Marriage Two

Two Weeks Later

Prince Harming and I flew out to Greece for our civil ceremony around a beautiful old village – the part that he had been yearning for. I wasn't one bit interested in his lavish plans but our closest friends had been invited and my sister had travelled from the UK, so it was all under way. Prince Harming hired a boat, a harpist and a beautiful old building was arranged in a pretty location so we could all walk through the town to the wedding venue and feel immersed in Greek culture.

We had a big dinner with all our guests the night before the wedding. I sat there thinking that I couldn't go through with the wedding. In my mind, Islamic marriage hadn't been valid, so I could still get out of it, but I was about to get *legally* married. Something in the pit of my stomach kept churning, making me feel that something was not right. I wish I had listened to that feeling instead of letting my head take over.

'I can't do this. I can't go through with this,' I told him.

He talked me around, made me feel safe.

We went to the ceremony venue the following day, but I was fifty-fifty as to whether I would actually go ahead with it because part of me knew I would be fully disconnected from my parents if I proceeded. I also did not trust him. Overwhelming butterflies (which I often get when I am scared) fluttered in my stomach. I wanted to get it over and done with and go back to my usual day-to-day life. I didn't trust him after he had been caught with his pants down with the air hostess barely a few months before. He had never really apologised or taken full responsibility for what he had done. A part of me didn't want to accept that he was like that. Perhaps he had learnt from his mistake? Perhaps he had changed? My head kept on spinning, I was too far down the road to pull out. My parents were also not speaking with me.... If only I'd had the strength and sense back then that I have now.

All I can say is that it wasn't a joyful day, lacking the excitement that anyone should have on their wedding day. I was riddled with anxiety. Even Prince Harming behaved as if someone had died, rather than being jubilant, loving and excited about the whole journey we were about to embark on.

The following day, the 'celebrations' with our friends continued and they then flew back home – leaving us on our own in Greece. Even then, we weren't gelling. We were seemingly floating on in our individual existences.

10

Early Married Life

The humdrum of life continued. Him working. Me working. An undercurrent of unease lapping beneath us. I still didn't trust him. Trust once lost is difficult to regain.

Barely six months passed before Prince Harming started lashing out at me when something didn't go his way. I didn't even know what I had done wrong half the time and I did not even notice the point when Prince Charming and switched to Prince Harming, it was gradual and was creeping up on me without me knowing because of the confused emotions and behaviour he would display towards me. Sometimes, however, he was very attentive; particularly when people were around us. He love-bombed me in front of others, after one of his usual outbursts he would send SMS messages stating the opposite of what had just happened and either stating he loved me, or that I was crazy and that he forgives me – this process of SMS'ing the opposite of what actually happened continued – until by magic years of SMS's (as if planned) appeared in court submissions many years later whilst I had little evidence of his outbursts towards me!.

The best way of abusing a woman seems to be to document each outburst in the opposite of what actually happened – a woman in the midst of this confused state of abuse will barely be able to stand up or be able to think, let alone 'plan' and 'document' incidents whilst they are happening!

It was when the doors closed at home that his male chauvinism crept out of the woodwork and I started seeing how I was suddenly, now that we were married, his possession, with expectations and duties as a wife. I still just looked at his behaviour towards me as culture.

'I'm the man. I'm the head of the family, and you need to know your place. You are married now and my family comes first.'

We had to spend more and more time with his family now that we were married. I was his wife. His tradition started creeping into our lives but only in the presence of certain people.

This was when I noticed that Prince Harming was two men: one who went out to get drunk and live the high life with his friends; and one who became the perfect Muslim man in front of his family.

He bossed me around and treated me 'like a woman should be treated'. To me, it was like he had a split personality. In his family's eyes, he behaved like a dominant man and I was expected to behave like an obedient wife… otherwise any wrong move could result in an outburst of abuse. I ended up living in a state of constant confusion and anxiety not knowing when the next outburst may come or why.

The cultural differences were alarming, and I realised that I hadn't known any of his life because we hadn't met each other's families properly before marrying. I didn't know his culture.

We lived worlds apart. The wife he wanted me to be was not who I was; I was always respectful to others, but I was independent. I had my own life. I made my own living. I didn't need a man, at least I didn't think I did. But I was now married and that meant moulding to his life, his family, and his traditions. Looking from the outside in – it looked great, nice house, nice cars, we looked like we had it all- yet behind those doors of those cars, of that house it was hell, trying to stand still on ground that was constantly shaking.

11

Losing and Gaining Financial Control

Sixteen Years Ago

Prince Harming decided that I would leave my prominent job to set up a business in our joint names. He had found an investor (whom he did legal work for) and asked him for seed money to set us up independently. With the capital in place, I handed my notice to my employers, who tried to keep me for another year. Prince Harming wouldn't accept that, so I left. I was scared because I had always had a stable job with prominent companies, and there I was, in a relatively foreign country, setting up a business.

Thankfully, I knew my business inside out, so we set up the company under both our names. Even so, I was the one at the forefront of the business. Everything had happened so quickly that I had clients on the day we opened for business and I had to meet in coffee shops because we didn't have an office.

Despite me taking the lead on everything, Prince Harming constantly reminded me that he was more important than me. And yet, I was doing all of the work… Put it this way, when his name was put forward to the relevant authority he was rejected a couple of times and only accepted when I put him under my supervision. And yet, he constantly put me down.

Prince Harming continued working at the law firm but managed our business's books, not allowing me to learn or look – even though I tried a number of times, 'finances are a man's job- you are not good with numbers' I would be told or accused of not trusting him. Ten years later, I know what that meant!

Meanwhile, I built up the client base. I worked all hours.

In the evenings, Prince Harming went out hobnobbing with his friends while I worked late – having nothing else to do

Fifteen Years Ago

Financial problems hit the global economy, which led to issues for many people, including the investor and potentially Prince Harming's connection to him. So, Prince Harming skipped town to set up an office in Far East Asia while things cooled down. From that moment on, he was barely living at home.

Our relationship was bad and things started getting worse.

During this time, he decided to launch a boutique hotel in the Indian Ocean and built the project from Far East Asia (notwithstanding that the Middle East was much closer to the proposed hotel!). He was living his life and using money earned from the business to build a boutique hotel with no connection to the business.

I am in no doubt that he was womanizing again because there were countless times that he inadvertently showed me pictures of his travels and a woman's body had been badly cropped from images, leaving, for example, an unexplainable well-manicured hand holding a glass in the image. When I questioned him on those occasions, he would say, 'It's in your head, it's in your head!' or 'Due to your fucked up upbringing you are suspicious.'

Being sworn at repeatedly was my norm, I was sworn at, my family was sworn at and I was constantly made to feel disgusting, a burden, a nuisance and reminded that I was nothing without him. I was, of course, told to never to turn up unplanned, so I would only travel in and out of his new home with his prior agreement.

12

Young Family Life…

Fourteen Years Ago

I telephoned Prince Harming in his Far East Asian home to let him know that we were expecting our first child. No response came from the other end of the line. It was as if I had told him that someone had died. Until I heard his reaction, or lack thereof, I had been over the moon about having a child.

There I was, alone, going to check-ups on my own. Prince Harming flew in and out to visit occasionally, but my trips to the Far East were scarce because he wanted plenty of notice before I visited. I wonder why.

Heavily pregnant and managing all business operations alone, I called and asked him to help.

'Don't tell me what to do, we have talked about this and agreed how things are done. Stop moving the goal posts. Stop taking away my dreams!' he shouted down the telephone.

And so it continued…

It was decided that I would have our child in the Far East, so I flew in and out for check-ups with Prince Harming's chosen gynaecologist. Otherwise, I continued a lone existence in the

Middle East: managing the business, our home, and carrying our baby.

Finally, our son, Mikel was born. We were both thrilled that we had a healthy baby, but Prince Harming had to head back to the Indian Ocean to continue his hotel project a few days later. Thankfully, my non-Muslim sister flew in from London and helped me out. (Prince Harming would use her religion against me in Sharia court in later years.)

I immediately knew that my husband had no interest in family life, once again learning that he didn't care one little bit. He twisted everything to make me feel like there was something wrong with me. I was, apparently, doing something wrong, asking too many questions, restricting his freedom by asking him to spend time with his family…..

Two days after returning home from the delivery of my son, I was back running the business with my sister helping me with Mikel in the early days – I had no one else to turn to.

Easter

I flew back to the Middle East with Prince Harming and Mikel after completing Mikel's first set of vaccinations. We had barely settled into life before Prince Harming headed off again. Thankfully, being excited to have a grandchild and putting aside some of the displeasure at my marriage, my mother flew over from the UK and helped for a month. So, I wasn't entirely alone managing everything with a new-born, including breast-feeding and pumping milk for my baby whilst working and managing the home and business.

One evening, when Prince Harming was in town, my mother offered to babysit so we could go out. We were barely seated in the restaurant when he said, 'I'm not sure about this whole kid thing, you have ruined my life by having a child. You've taken away my dreams. I don't know why people think having kids is amazing. It's not for me.'

'Our son is barely a few weeks old and you're telling me you don't 'feel' it'?!' I was astonished at what I was hearing.

His reaction, on top of managing everything else, triggered post-natal depression, though I did not recognise it at the time. (It was also raised by Prince Harming as an indication of some negative psychological disposition in the UK courts later) I just carried on looking after the home, the business, and our new-born child.I knew then that I had f***ed up my life BIG time- but almost afraid of acknowledging this to myself.

Thirteen Years Ago

Prince Harming continued travelling a lot. I was living in the Middle East. We lived separate lives.

I had to pre-book if I wanted to visit him in the Far East.

If I asked him anything at all he would remind me:

'You don't know what you're asking!'

'You don't fucking appreciate me!'

'Don't tell me what I can and can't do!'

'Why can't you just let me be?!'

It got worse and worse and worse. I felt as though I was constantly treading on eggshells; not doing this, doing that, making sure work was done, looking after the house, making certain not to look at him the wrong way… I was helpless.

'You're not focusing enough on the business since having the baby; we're not making enough money!'

So, I stepped up my workload.

I was constantly living on the edge of an abyss. In a cycle of abuse without knowing it was abuse.

It was hell.

I stopped saying anything at all. I was terrified. But I normalised it. And there was no one I could reach out to you – that nice house, those cars is all people saw, not the pain inside.

13

Mikel Being Hospitalised

Eleven Years Ago

Three months into the pregnancy with our second child, Mikel, barely a toddler, was hospitalised with a convulsion when my mother was visiting. His face turned pale, his lips went blue, his eyes rolling into the back of his head. Prince Harming was in the UK with his family, so I had to call for an ambulance. I didn't even know how to do that in a foreign country because they were asking which hospital we wanted to go to. Apparently, it was dependant on our insurance. I didn't even know if we had insurance because Prince Harming controlled everything as the children's visa sponsor.

We finally went to a government hospital, but it transpired that Prince Harming, being Mikel's visa sponsor, had not arranged insurance. I didn't have any money for my son's admission, so I tried ringing Prince Harming so he could pay me my 'salary'. (Yes, even though we had a joint business, he would drip feed me a 'monthly salary' causing me to be in overdraft for nearly ten years.)

No reply.

I tried again.

No reply.

When he eventually phoned back, he told me he would travel to the Middle East as soon as he could, but that he had a family matter to deal with first. He would fly in the following day – after Mikel's admission, diagnosis and treatment – hardly high priority.

With little option, I went into my office and took the petty cash from the safe so that I could pay for my son's admission, telling my staff I had left my wallet at home. The office was closer to the hospital. I was waiting for two days for Prince Harming to pay me my 'salary' for the business I managed. There I was, well into my overdraft, with a two-year-old son and three months into pregnancy, in a hospital in a foreign country.

My life was pretty shit.

When Prince Harming arrived a few days later, he went home for a shower and a change of clothes before coming to visit. He then popped in for a few hours before going home to sleep. I stayed in the hospital with my son for seven days. My Mum also stayed overnight with my son and I in hospital. Prince Harming, meanwhile, preferred to sleep in the comfort of his own bed.

I was embarrassed that my mum was witnessing me alone in hospital with our son, all while I was three months pregnant. It's pretty hard to hide the reality of your broken life when it plays out in front of people but, under the shroud of culture, we were left to our own devices.

14

Quicksand

Whilst pregnant with our second child, Prince Harming decided he wanted our daughter to be born in London. He wanted us to be around his family. He had since left the Far East and was now spending time between Coventry and Latin America where – wait for it – he was 'building a hotel'. This was a different one – I never quite understood what happened to the hotel in Indian Ocean and nor was I allowed to ask.

That Summer we travelled to our apartment in London ahead of the birth and my sister came to babysit my son ahead of the planned delivery the following day.

'I don't trust my husband, I am not happy,' I told her, 'Surely you also wonder why he is spending so much time in Latin America, Far East and not at home?'

I now know that he had a separate life over there, with the woman who is now his wife. My sister doubted it was possible – why I don't know, maybe because from the outside in- everything looked great, and Prince Harming would always be publicly charming. Then again, everyone doubted me because Prince Harming was a manipulative master of disguise.

Defeated again by my sisters response, feeling unheard and disbelieved...again, I headed to hospital in the morning for the scheduled delivery. Prince Harming disappeared for about four hours during labour to have a sandwich and turned up just in time for the birth. Prince Harming then left us to it until my sister asked to visit the hospital. Like clockwork, Prince Harming returned with flowers and chocolates – showing everybody what an attentive husband he was.

Again, however, it was like he was grieving at the thought of another child. He later told me that having any more children would be the end of our marriage…diverting attention away from him to his children was not acceptable.

Upon discharge, we stayed in our London apartment for one week while I was recovering and for the midwife to do her home visit, so I sat caring for our baby and replying to emails on my Blackberry. Prince Harming did not give a shit. In his mind, a man is a man and family comes after him…

That was my life.

We travelled from London to Coventry to spend time with Prince Harming's family one week after the baby was born. We were told to stay at his sister's house, who, although pleasant, likes keeping her house immaculately clean. Being post-partum, with a new-born, a toddler, and a business to manage, that was hardly a restful place. This was then followed by the hospitalisation of my father who was admitted to hospital with an infectious disease. I travelled with my children to see him but wasn't allowed in for long because he was potentially highly contagious. So, I saw him through a glass screen for a few days and then travelled back to Coventry to tell Prince Harming that I wanted to go home to the Middle East – to my own space and to get the kids settled, everything was just too much. There were too many things happening at the same time. It was emotionally draining. I just wanted to go home.

Our baby was only a few weeks old, resting in a sling on my chest when I asked him to let us go home.

*'You can't f*cking go home. You're using my family and we will go home when we say we will.'*

I'll never forget him shouting at me while I held our baby in her sling. I'd had enough and retaliated, telling him where to go in no uncertain terms.

'WHAT DID YOU FUCKING SAY?!' Prince Harming screamed at me in front of his sister and her husband. It terrified me, so I starting running up the stairs to get away from him. He followed me, shouting repeatedly at me as I starting speeding up the stairs and rushing to get into the room we were staying in. I knew it had a lock on the door, but I did not manage to lock it in time.

I was broken.

That very evening the rest of Prince Harming's family turned up to go out for a charity dinner, and it was as if nothing had happened. Many an occasion arose where onlookers looked away because it was a domestic matter, or I would be told that I must have done something to cause Prince Harming's behaviour towards me; or the usual response: I chose to marry him, so now I had to deal with it.

When his family arrived, I was still hiding upstairs, terrified, thinking that them leaving the house together might be my chance to escape. As soon as I heard the front door close, I went downstairs to find they had left one of the sister's kids with me, and the keys to our hire car were nowhere to be found.

There was no chance of escape.

Looking back, I wish I had called someone in my family at that point to come clean about his aggressive, manipulative and controlling behaviour. But I was worried about the anticipated reaction I usually got from both families: I chose to marry him, had made my bed, so now should lie in it.

The following day, Prince Harming asked to speak to me – I was terrified not knowing his next reaction. He sat down with me and said, 'I don't know what had happened or why we fought like that yesterday, but I forgive you. Let's just move forward.'

'YOU FORGIVE ME?!' I thought.

In my head, I pondered whether this guy was for real. I was unable to respond and my delay angered him again. His ranting started again.

'You can't move forward; you are always holding onto things. Just draw a line and move forward for God's sake!'

Things like this happened all the time but I had learnt to nod and agree to whatever he was rambling on about, just to get him to shut up and go away. My newest survival rule was to nod, agree and remove myself to do my best to avoid being alone with him. In most cases I don't even know what I had nodded to, it was an automated response I triggered to make him stop shouting at me, to go away, but his usual follow on SMS would remind me of his view of what happened even if completely different to what actually happened. He was a master at deflecting and blaming me for the very thing he was doing to me. Then, to top it off, he would end by telling me he forgave me! We were living in his 'reality' and it was scary, confusing and constantly unstable.

15

A Dark Hole

Ten Years Ago

You've probably got the gist of things now; life was miserable. Settling back into Middle Eastern life, it was all the same story, only with fewer prying eyes to keep Prince Harming somewhat under control. Our life was a merry-go-round. We were back and forth from the Middle East to Coventry – running a business – spending time with his family – more running of the business – looking after the children… Abuse. Prince Harming was doing whatever he wanted to do; travelling between Latin America, London, the Middle East and Coventry; and wherever else he wanted to go and with whomever he wanted to go with.

Blame. Abuse. Shouting. Deflection. Control. Blame. Abuse. Shouting. Deflection. Control. It went on and on and on and on and on….

I mustered up the courage to tell him to stop on a couple of occasions, telling him I couldn't carry on living in that hell, but I was swiftly reminded of where we were:

'You can't do anything to me because I'm a Muslim man in a Muslim country,' Prince Harming informed me, 'Under Sharia Law, I have all the say. If you leave me, I get the kids, the house – I get everything. DON'T EVEN THINK ABOUT IT.'

He wasn't wrong; it would be extremely difficult to leave him. I had long expected I would one day find proof of an extra-marital relationship with somebody in Latin America, but even that wouldn't be grounds for divorce because multiple marriages were permitted where we lived.

I had to find another way out and ignore the lingering thought that I may be stuck in this hell hole forever. Losing hope would destroy me.

In the meantime, I found ways to cope:

- **Coping Mechanism Number One:** Don't speak.
- **Coping Mechanism Number Two:** Don't look at him. Because if you do look at him, you might look at him the wrong way and that will set him off.
- **Coping Mechanism Number Three:** Avoid eye contact and cover face with hair so facial expressions cannot be seen just in case you make a gesture he does not like without realising.
- **Coping Mechanism Number Four:** Speak only when spoken to and keep conversation very brief: 'Yes, you are right,' being the safest response.

16

A Family Lunch

Nine Years Ago

On one rare occasion, when my daughter was about four, Prince Harming's nephew, who had also moved to the Middle East from Coventry and was put in the joint business as an employee witnessed one of our 'moments'. I had asked Prince Harming if he could stop texting at the table. His hand was carefully shielding his phone. I wanted him to engage with the children because he had been ignoring them throughout lunch. He had just come back from Latin America and we were supposed to be enjoying a rare family meal in a restaurant.

Prince Harming gave me 'the death stare' in reply. My heart sank as I knew I would be in for the usual 'special treatment'. As always, I was unsure when it would come. That all too familiar churning in my stomach started.

Having shown his displeasure, Prince Harming told us to hurry up so lunch could finish, and that we should go immediately home. We sat in silence while the bill came. Then, we were leaving the restaurant when Prince Harming slowed me down and took me aside to warn me to stop 'this behaviour'. He reminded me that he could do whatever he wanted, that I was suffocating him, that I didn't 'let him be'.

I hung my head down in shame as he walked ahead to catch up with his nephew.

At home he reminded me in no uncertain and very loud terms that: *'I am fucking independent and can do whatever I want. If you don't like that, you are not good enough for me!!'*

I was fed up and accidentally brushed past him as I moved to run upstairs. This caused a greater outburst of anger. Prince Harming followed, constantly shouting at me. I kept running upstairs. He was cursing, raising his voice higher to ensure I heard him.

God, I heard him the first time.

I had done something he didn't like, clearly, but I had no idea what it was. Prince Harming followed me to my escape room (my bedroom). He locked the door behind him so I couldn't leave until he did 'all he wanted to'. He spat, screamed, shouted, standing over me to intimidate me. The usual.

I couldn't take it anymore.

I screamed back and told him I couldn't live in this hell. I then tried to get the bedroom keys that he had put in his pocket. I remember very clearly; he wore those beige cargo pants with pockets along both legs. The keys were in one of the side pockets. But when I attempted to grab them, he kept turning and moving to avoid me getting them.

I got dizzy from trying to get the keys, and I fell. He took this opportunity to kick me. Lying there, I was horrified at where my life had ended up. I got up and pushed him away from me- when you feel you have nothing left, no hope – you break

'This is enough, enough!' I screamed, *'Let me go, let me out of this living hell!!!'*

Prince Harming opened the door, walked out and headed out of the house with his nephew as if nothing has happened. When the children checked that he had gone and it was safe, they came to sit with me – one wiping my tears and the other holding my arm to comfort me. I sobbed in utter despair.

'I am in a fucking black hole,' I thought, 'With two kids depending on me. I can't find my way out. I wish I was dead.'

17

Lump Number One

Nine Years Ago

Weeks and years seem to go by with the unpredictable outbursts increasing causing me to feel anxiety and frequent tightening of my chest. To top it all, I noticed a disturbing lump in one of my breasts and telephoned Prince Harming who was as usual, out of the country somewhere, to tell him I was worried about it, but he told me it was all in my head. It was the same old story. Putting me down. Making me think that perhaps it was in my head and he did not want to be disturbed whilst travelling. Was it in my head?!

I took myself to a doctor who referred me for a scan. They found a lump, took a scan and found it wasn't anything to worry about. I was sent home with a deferred check-up one year later.

To be honest, for a time I wasn't worried if the breast lump worsened. I figured that perhaps it might be a way out of the hell I was living in. Then, however, my maternal brain stepped in and told me I had to be OK – if only for my children – so I started worrying again: What will happen to my children if something happens to me?

So, the lump was kept under review and would lead to a future biopsy. But it didn't end there. It also led to a later car spin off and, of course, abuse.

18

The Cinema Outburst

Eight Years Ago

On another rare occasion, we had agreed to meet Prince Harming at the cinema with the children. He would travel on his own, liking his privacy so, the kids and I took our own car. We reached the shopping mall, Nysa still in her stroller and Mikel, no older than four or five, walking alongside me towards the cinema. Mikel and I select movies from the cinema board and then choose the snacks we are going to eat. Then, Prince Harming arriving late, as he usually did, and automatically dictates what we will watch. We try to explain what we wanted to watch, but that starts the abuse, the rage, the shouting. I should have known not to disagree with him. I should have adopted Coping Mechanism Number Four.

To be honest, by this time I had no idea what and when he would go on a rampage, but I recognised that tone in his voice, his body language, that look on his face, and then the rage.

He's ranting at full volume in the cinema foyer, with people looking on whilst my son and I hang our heads down, my daughter hiding her face in her stroller. Shamed. People stop to look until Prince Harming shouts at those complete strangers to demand they stop looking.

This, apparently, is a family matter and it is none of anyone's business. They turn away. *They always turn away.*

The cinema's security guard has now come to our rescue and is asking Prince Harming to lower his voice, but Prince Harming is not a man to be told what to do. He snaps back at the security guard. At least the rage is now on somebody else. But I'm mortified.

Still, the security guard was our saviour. Although slightly shorter than Prince Harming, he remains standing near the children and me until Prince Harming eventually starts moving back. But he now tries to remove Mikel from me by tugging his arm who clings even more tightly to his sister's pushchair – all in plain sight of the security guard.

Eventually, Prince Harming walks off ranting as he goes. I sink to the floor to hide in shame behind my daughter's stroller.

The security guard hands Mikel a box of tissues, who takes one for me to wipe my tears away. I feel devastated and trapped but these two children of mine are looking at me, willing me to get up, so I do. We are welcomed into a coffee shop opposite the cinema entrance. The staff obviously witnessed the outburst. We sit down in complete numbness. They ask me if I want something and I don't know what to answer. In their kindness they give my children a cookie whilst I try to comprehend what has happened and what to do next. Will Prince Harming be waiting at home?...will I get the usual abuse as soon as we go home?

I stay in the coffee shop for a few moments to take in the peace.

By this point, the outbursts we had been accustomed to in private began to seep more regularly into public settings. Many a bystander looked on until they were told to 'mind their own business' or that it was 'a family matter', and they always moved on. I wish just one of those bystanders had ignored Prince Harming, perhaps called help for us, but they did not.

19

The Teller

Seven Years Ago

I was constantly living deep into an overdraft, being drip-fed my 'salary' while dealing with the stress of worrying about the breast lump, work, and caring for two children and dealing with Prince Harming and his unpredictable outbursts in a constant state of anxiety with relief when he was travelling.

Enough was enough. If I didn't do something, I WOULD die, the stress and anxiety of living with this Jekyll and Hyde was taking its toll.

I had some idea of the money I was bringing into our business, so I thought it was about time I went to get some of the money that Prince Harming had always denied me. At this point he had started repairs in the house and left them unfinished, telling me we did not have enough money and so many expenses that he had to wear shoes with broken soles and drive a hire car. Like an idiot, I believed him. Nor did I have the emotional strength to challenge him. In my mind, I didn't understand why he would leave ceilings and AC systems broken all year when temperatures reach 50 degrees in Summer, particularly when he had a child with severe eczema, surely he would not pretend…?

'An abuser may not work but instead live off a victim-survivor, giving the impression of working but actually contributing little. For example, this may take place through a joint business venture. Here an abuser often creates a situation where the victim-survivor is working constantly to pay off debts and bills, while earning money to stay alive, which can lead to dependence and/or exhaustion.'

UK Economic Abuse Toolkit- Example[15]

Late in Spring, I approached the bank with my trade licence showing fifty percent ownership of the company and my passport in hand, I went to the bank and took a ticket to wait my turn to see a teller.

My number was called, and I asked the teller if I could make a withdrawal. Sounds simple, right?

The teller did what all tellers do, punching numbers into her computer (it always seems like they are doing more than they should have to do to access money, doesn't it?).

'Don't you have an ATM card to make withdrawals, Madam?' the teller then asked.

'No, I didn't know you could have an ATM card on a business account.'

'There's an ATM card registered to this account.'

I had no idea what she was talking about.

'OK, please take a seat over there and I should be able to assist you when I've spoken to your Relationship Manager.' I took a seat for another fifteen minutes before my name was called again.

'OK, Madam, how much do you want?' the teller asked. I pause and stutter not knowing what to ask or how much?

The teller asks again. 'Madam, how much would you like, 10,000, 20,000... or more?'

'Please can I withdraw 10,000 dollars?'

'You can take more if you want?' she said when she saw the excitement on my face.

I was so nervous that I told her 10,000 was plenty as I had no clue how much money was in the accounts.

She took my chequebook and entered all of the information so that I could then take a cheque to a machine to clear the money, which would then be transferred to my personal account. I can't explain how freeing that felt.

I had done it. I was liberated. Perhaps I could actually find my way out of this relationship by saving money – until I had enough to leave. Hopes and dreams flowed through my head, and I rushed home grinning from cheek to cheek when thinking about freedom. I didn't really know what I was doing, but it felt great.

I opened the front door to see Prince Harming eating his breakfast at the head of the dining room table, in the middle of the day. He never surfaced until about eleven in the morning, but I was not expecting him to be there. How was I going to hide the smile on my face? How was I going to hide what I had just done behind his back? I started shaking from fear.

Surely it would make him angry if he found out.

Surely…

'Where have you been?'

'Nowhere,' I replied. Oh shit, he knows something, I thought. No, he can't. That's impossible.

'Sit down.'

I sat down.

'I am not going to get angry but I know where you have been. You went to the bank at eleven o'clock this morning and at eleven-fifteen you asked a teller to withdraw 10,000 dollars from our business account. Do you know what happened next? They called me,' he said with a straight, unwavering face.

My face dropped with the realisation that I was entirely trapped. I was sure I was going to get hit, screamed at, cursed at, locked in a room, or a combination of them all...

Very calmly, Prince Harming looked right at me and told me 'I'm not going to get angry with you, but you have to give that money back,' he said, his words worse than a beating, sending a shiver down my spine.

'I need some money to pay the bills and get out of my overdraft.'

'OK, I will let you keep 3,000 dollars but you need to give the rest back,'

He then took my chequebook from me and wrote out a cheque from my account for 7,000 dollars to be made payable back into the main business account – the account I had no access to.

'Don't do it again, because I will be notified every time you go in. I won't stand for it.' He got up and left.

His words finalised our conversation and I was left coming

to the abrupt realisation that he controlled everything. I was devastated. It felt like the ground underneath me had just disappeared.

There was no way I could gather enough money to leave.

I was entirely dependent on Prince Harming drip-feeding my salary when he wanted and I had to keep working to pay the bills and expenses for the children. I was trapped.

It is not clear if the global bank concerned or its relationship managers breached any confidentiality requirements or vulnerability codes? I wonder how many women have been beaten or abused by their partners as a result of such bank staff sharing information? It's a good job that there was no accountability or code of conduct that needed to be followed(!)

From that day onwards, I felt dead. Empty. I carried on because I had no choice, but I wasn't present. I had lost all sense of hope, stuck in a marriage to a man I had chosen against my parents' wishes: I had made my bed, now had to lie or die in it!

I finally realised: I had married a monster.

20

Why Did I Not Just Leave?

Here is a question many women in abusive relationships will hear at some point: *why did you just not leave?* The better question to ask is *'Why did you stay?'*, There may be a number of reasons, individually or collectively but I describe it as living in an open jail.

Let me explain.

Shame, Society And Culture

I was raised in a culture where dating prior to marriage was not permitted. Combined with seeing my father shout and abuse my mother – it was all 'normal' and coupled with ' he will calm down', ' stay out of his way', ' don't do anything to make him angry' – that is how we were raised. One glance from my father was enough to silence a room, especially my mother who through religion and social expectation would never have challenged my father let alone have expected to consider leaving her marriage.

To look at my mother's achievements you would only see a strong woman – she worked, had her own car, unlike many women of her generation – but she accepted the abuse. She had no choice.

A generation later – my turn – whilst I made choices, my life started mirroring my mother, except I had chosen my own partner, a Muslim man which was taboo across our culture. After the upheaval caused by choosing Prince Charming, how could I return to my family admitting what was happening? I was not even sure that door would still be open for me especially after having children – how would I be perceived as a single mother choosing to marry a man of a different religion and background? Combine this with no access to financial resources, living in a Muslim country and married to a Muslim man.

Is It Abuse?

When you have normalised the experiences in your life, you don't always realise it is wrong especially when it has not stopped or been stopped by others. What makes this state of confusion worse is the belief that non-physical abuse is not domestic abuse, right? I did not even consider that I was in a domestically abusive relationship because it was predominantly non-physical abuse with only occasional instances of physical abuse.

But I was, subjected to constant verbal abuse, locked in rooms, and experiencing persistent intimidating, coercive and aggressive behaviour compounded by family members 'condoning' Prince Harming's behaviour, blaming me for his outbursts or by normalising his behaviour by telling me it was all OK, that his behaviour was not that bad, or that he was just angry or upset. It felt bad and I knew it wasn't right, but I was confused.

That all changed when he kicked me after I fell to the floor attempting to get the keys from him to get out of the locked room.

Perhaps if there was more physical abuse, I may have felt the urgency to leave sooner. Or perhaps if someone had explicitly reached out to help me. I had to get out of the life we were in because of the anxiety, the breast lump, constant pains across my chess, inability to sleep and constant fear that was caused by what was happening even if I could not give it a label or a description.

And incredulously, it wasn't until much, much later that I began to understand that none of what was happening was my fault. But when you are subjected to *daily* abuse – physical or non-physical – you normalise the abuse and constantly walking on eggshells not knowing when the next outburst will happen. You normalise becoming hyper-vigilant. And you normalise detaching your emotions – dissociating from the abuse – in order to cope.

I was so used to him shouting and not letting me speak that I became known for speaking very fast, almost like trying to squeeze as many words in as possible before I would be stopped but no-one knew why. No-one knew I would be locked in rooms, not allowed to speak, and not allowed to leave.

Non-physical abuse does not leave bruises or scars but it does wound you internally. You are under so much psychological and emotional stress that it stops you thinking. You are unable to make simple decisions because the part of your brain that solves problems is literally offline. You are in survival mode.

I have been told that perhaps due to years of looking over my shoulder, walking on eggshells and not being able to make it stop, and from the impact of being detained in locked rooms the effect has been quite profound. I have been told that I *still* present with symptoms of Post-Traumatic Stress Disorder (PTSD).

When I finally moved into my own home in the UK, I removed all the bedroom doors. I could not bear to be locked in. My own bedroom has no curtains, because I need to see the outside – a way out.

Gradual Erosion Of A Social Network

As with other women, I became isolated from my friends through a combination of Prince Harming confusing me with public 'love-bombing' and charming and engaging conversations with my friends showing a caring and intelligent ma; and my own self-caution due to Prince Harming convincing me that my friends were talking behind my back... and coming to him complaining about me. It became easier and more peaceful to stay alone. I could not trust anyone. He had turned members of my own family against me by showering them with gifts. While they saw a business woman, they did not see that he controlled the finances completely. No-one knew that I was living on a meagre survival budget surviving on the overdraft.

Financially, I could not get out.

'Smart Women Don't Get Abused? Right?'

This is the ultimate irony. Professionally, on the outside, I was very well known I had a good career, and job stability. I was qualified and good at my job.

My job was my safety net. Keeping my mind and focus on work kept my mind away from thinking about what was happening to my children and I at home. I was expected to go to work and be at home by a certain time or else account for my day. There was no out-of-hours socialising. And who would believe me?

So I had a *work face* where everything is fine.

You are thinking: educated women don't get abused, right? Wrong. I even thought that! That doubt lead to even more reluctance to speak out. People still express disbelief. 'Why you did not realise this was happening when you are so smart?'

I was smart at my job. Professionally I was well respected but at home I was told I was worthless, disliked, and sworn at frequently- my job was the only place I had value, I had worth where I could solve a problem, a place I did not have to be 'me'. But domestic abuse is not just one factor. It was multiple factors – subtle and explicit – that kept me – and anyone – trapped in that situation.

No Financial Resources

Access to money was restricted. My money being drip fed to me and I lived in a country where banks have no obligations regarding economic abuse. And I had to support my children – they were used as weapons to control me, ensuring I kept working to support them. How would I leave with no funds to survive or support my children?

Children

Another consideration remained. My young children: what would be the impact on them if we left? Would I be OK on my own with them? But this thought about keeping the family together became overshadowed by the environment the children were living in, and what they were exposed to.

When women finally decide to leave, they may have no emotional strength to do so, or financial resources. An added complexity related to visa and sponsorship rules in certain countries – my children were under the visa sponsorship of their father so I was not even sure how that would pan out in a divorce – would I be able to sponsor them? How would custody arrangements work? The fear of losing the custody of your children is perhaps one of the most crippling thoughts you go through and one of the biggest reasons for staying in an abusive relationship.

When my children became hyper-vigilant, acting as my caretakers and the concern that their role models would be an abusive father and mother who tolerated it gave me the focus to get out. My life had begun to mirror my mother's. I did not want my son to grow up thinking it is OK to treat women like this and nor did I want my daughter to have a limited expectation of her life. I did not want my life to be echoed in my children's.

Fear and Control

Ultimately, you are afraid. I had been threatened with so many things – religion, culture, custody – that I was petrified. It was only the breast lump, and the bank incident that pushed me to take action. I was no longer able to normalise it. I was trapped and my health impacted.

He had taken everything from me, and it was from this point I worked hard to build my physical, emotional and financial strength to get myself and my children out of that hell even though I had no clue how I was going to do it, but I needed to get out. I used his abuse to help me stay focussed.

Even when you make the decision to go, racked with self-doubt, you rethink it hundreds of times. Will he change? Can it get better? Do I want to give up my marriage? What will people think? The biggest fear I had at this point was: if I don't succeed in getting away from him, what will he do to me, then?

I don't know how many times I asked my lawyers this question again and again to make sure they get me my divorce and custody of my children. The fear of returning to him was sickening.

Walk In My Shoes

For those who still ask the question, why did I not leave, I simply ask them to imagine being locked in a glass box with water being poured in gradually, before you know it you are struggling to keep your head above water and because you have been in that box for so long, it has become familiar and your only way of living... until you begin to drown. You either fight your way to get out or you succumb because you have been exhausted from treading water to keep your head above the water.

- Your friends and family gradually isolated from you.
- Your financial resources depleted and controlled.
- The loss of your children is used to threaten you.
- Your physical, emotionally strength destroyed.
- Your culture, society, religion normalising some aspects of your life and expectations on women.
- Disbelief stops you reaching out.
- Fear of repercussions from the abuser – especially if you fail to escape.

All or some of these result in women living in 'open jails' imprisoned in their own lives.

Speaking Out Makes It Real

Most importantly, when you finally speak out, it becomes 'real' something that can no longer be normalised, that is the most frightening part. When I look back at my journey, it still remains excruciatingly uncomfortable with some aspects still too overwhelming to process.

Whilst many professionals in the family justice system ignore domestic abuse when it is historical, or focus only on the most recent physical violence they ignore the impacts of the protracted trauma which has no clear end date.

No Information- Where Do I Go Next?

Like many women in my situation, you do not know what to do or how to get away safely. Some women have no job, no bank account, have not been permitted to make decisions. The fear of not knowing what do to may keep abused women in their 'open jails'.

I must have reached out to many in desperation to try to understand what I am meant to do to get out of the hell I was in and given contradictory information, or no information until I started researching the local family law and support agencies but it was very confusing, overwhelming that it took me several months to finally pluck up the courage to take that leap of faith and start my escape. I hope that the information that I have gathered over the last seven years and provided in this book may also help other women by providing some information that I wish I had been given.

Part 2

My Story: Getting Out

21

Wishful Thinking

Four Months Later

Following plenty of time processing my conversation with Prince Harming the day I had been to the bank, I wondered whether he had made it all up. Perhaps he had got lucky and guessed I had gone to the bank. Maybe a friend of his had seen me there that day and the bank hadn't actually called him. Had I believed him too easily? And I was at a point of utter despair and the feeling of being trapped was exhausting, like being in a maze and constantly hitting a dead end or overwhelmed as to which direction to attempt to go down to find your way.

Unsure and hopeful that I had jumped to the wrong conclusion, I decided to go back to the bank to withdraw money – wishing that I would gather enough to escape.

I arrived at the bank and followed the same routine as the previous time. 'Please take a seat Madam so we can call the relationship manager.'

I sat in the same reception area until this time Prince Harming telephoned me and said, 'I know where you are. You can't get access to that money, stop trying.'

My worst fears were indeed true.

I started screaming in the bank and all the way out of it. I screamed throughout the taxi journey home. *Let me go, let me go, let me go!!!*

Tears rolling down my face, suffocating in the feeling of being trapped in an open jail. That feeling of screaming but no sound coming out, no-one can hear you...

I was worse than dead – trapped in a life I hadn't chosen.

22

The Beginning of the End

The Biopsy

Two months later I was called back for my annual check-up on my breast lump and was told that it had changed shape and that I needed a biopsy to ensure it was still benign.

Having considered all options, I decided I trusted the hospitals more in the UK, so Prince Harming and I travelled to Coventry together for my biopsy.

We stayed in our apartment in Coventry (having sold our London apartment to buy one near his family) where I was constantly being told off by Prince Harming for looking at him the *wrong* way, not looking at him the *right* way, looking up or looking down, not speaking up, speaking too much, speaking too little – I couldn't win, so stopped trying at this point.

After leaving the children with Prince Harming's mother, we got into the car and he starts his ranting, on and on and on…I don't even remember what I did wrong, perhaps just being alive was the reason. Of all days – he kept ranting as we were driving for my biopsy.

I stared out of the car window trying to block him out: another coping mechanism. I think I had not spoken to his mother correctly or not spoken enough. I had no idea what I did wrong and did not care.

I was heading for a biopsy. His ranting and voice droning on in the background. I was trying not to cry, just hoping we could get to the hospital soon (which we did as it was barely a ten-minute drive from the apartment). In my mind thoughts about the lump and if it could set me free – that way I can finally get away from this man and this life!

In the doctor's surgery, Prince Harming rubbed my arm as if he was a doting husband but I couldn't stand it, so I pushed him away. That instigated the doctor asking him to leave me alone. Perhaps, finally someone could actually see him for what he truly was.

I burst into tears and said, unusually for me, 'I want my mum.'

I was not even sure how I could approach my Mum; would she judge me and be difficult if I opened up about the marriage I was in? Either way, having him there was worse.

The examination proceeded.

I was numb.

The biopsy was benign, but I was told I should have regular mammograms because my cystic condition may be worsened by stress. No wonder.

On the way home, the ranting resumed.

I couldn't take any more, so I opened the car door to get out at the traffic light stop. There I was, with one leg out into the pouring rain, when Prince Harming accelerated. I was only halfway out of the car, so I stumbled out.

Déjà vu from the events that followed the standoff with Prince Harming and the air hostess!

I walked home alone. A fifteen-minute brisk walk.

Two days later, Prince Harming flew to Latin America. I flew back to the Middle East, a few days after the biopsy, with children in arms, our luggage and recovering from a core biopsy to get the children back to school. The wound became infected shortly after.

By then, my do-or-die instinct had finally been triggered. When you feel you have nothing left, you will try anything because staying where you are is terrifying.

Prince Harming's rationale for not needing to travel back with us was quite simple – we were separated at the time, living and sleeping in different rooms and he therefore had no duty towards me – his view, lack of empathy and comments being accepted by the UK family court in 2021.

> "For example, a matter of some significance to the mother is, she says, the father's callousness to her when a lump was found in her breast or when X had a febrile seizure... X. Illustrations, she says, of where the father failed and was more concerned about himself. But, having listened to his evidence, it was perfectly plain that what he told me was true. In fact, it seemed to me that he was genuinely anxious to assist his wife when she was unwell and genuinely anxious to get back to be with his son. He regretted, I thought genuinely, that she felt and feels the way that she did about those examples that she raised."

UK High Court Judge, Family Division, 2021, Parental Alienation decision against the mother in fact-finding hearing.

23

Family Dinner – Smiles On Please

Back in the Middle East, I received a call from Prince Harming: 'I am back from Latin America. My niece and her friend are coming for dinner. I will bring food. Just make sure you behave yourself. Fiona has been telling me what you have been up to, and I am not happy.'

My heart sinks because firstly, he's back from one of his trips; secondly, I don't know what the fuck I have done wrong now; and thirdly, I wonder when am I going to get my usual abusive outburst and ranting from him. My anxiety and stress triggered with his phone call.

I get home at the usual time after picking the children up from school and nursery. Our housekeeper, Fiona, is strutting around avoiding any eye contact with me (this is usual as she had more importance in the house than I did). I have no idea what they have been saying to each other as Fiona knew Prince Harming's travel plans more than I did. I avoid any unnecessary engagement until he comes home much later.

'What is this I hear? You have been meddling in other people's homes? Going out? Fiona told me everything.'

What the hell have I done, or what am I being blamed for now?

Shall I defend myself or just stay quiet and hope he will get tired and stop ranting?

'Speak up I can't hear you.'

'I- I- I didn't say anything...'

'Why can't you just be normal and not go to your friend's house and speak about family business?'

'I have not done anything,' I try to reply, but before I finish, the ranting starts, and it gets louder and louder. I head upstairs and hear him following, so I move faster to get up the stairs into the room where I can lock the door. He keeps coming and is now in the room. The door gets locked behind us and here we go again. He starts his ranting.

'You are fucking disgusting. Your family is fucked up, you are fucked up, a suspicious woman, out of control, everyone hates you…I am the only mug that will put up with you.'

I manage to get to the door. The key is in the lock, and I get out of the room to run downstairs, but he follows. He always follows. I run to the kitchen where Fiona is. Prince Harming now locks the kitchen door behind him. Now there are two of us being held captive and now he has his ally. I sit on the kitchen counter and run my hair over my face so he can't see my facial expressions (Coping Mechanism Number Three).

'Look at me when I'm talking to you!'

I keep looking down, hoping he will give up and go away.

But he keeps ranting and now… Not the gritting of teeth and snarling, not the foaming of the mouth again, please – not the foaming mouth.

Not the spit.

'You don't listen, you don't change!'

I just keep my head down and keep asking myself: 'What the fuck did I do wrong this time?!'

In his frustration, he uses his two fingers to keep pushing my forehead up to look up at him but I keep dropping my head down…and he keeps pushing my head up… again… and again. I don't deserve this.

Then, the doorbell rings, 'Pull yourself together, we've got guests.'

Five minutes later, we sit down for dinner with his niece and her friend. Prince Harming behaves as if nothing has just happened. I feel so physically sick that I can't eat. Prince Harming proceeds to serve my food in front of his guests.

'I don't know what to do with your aunt,' he tells his niece, 'nothing is good enough for her. I am doing my best for the family but it's not good enough for her,' he continues, as he puts on a sympathetic face to seek sympathy.

I pick at my food when he turns to me and asks me why am I not eating. He asks me what is wrong with the food that he had specially ordered for me. I continue to play with the food while he engages with his niece and friend, advising them where to go to see the best sights. Always Mr Engaging and Mr Interesting for his guests – the public showman, the 'Jekyll and Hyde'.

Dinner finally ends, and Prince Harming drives them back to their hotel, so I immediately run to my room.

Coping Mechanism Number Five: Duplicate all keys to the doors in the house so I can lock myself in the room and stay there out of harm's way. And sleep with keys under my pillow so I don't lose sight of them – they are my lifeline. Don't forget to lock the door before falling asleep.

I am alone in that room with my kids (my children and I would typically lock ourselves in my bedroom after dinner each night to keep safe).

The key is my saviour, even if nobody can see what was happening to me. At least I am safely locked away.

Oh shit, I forgot to lock the door. The door bursts open. Prince Harming is home from dropping his niece and her friend home.

'Don't you ever embarrass me like that again! How dare you. You're disgusting.'

I interrupt Prince Harming and say, 'Shall I finish your sentences? I know exactly what you are going to say to me. It's the same every time.' His ranting goes on. I look down and try to ignore him.

'Look at me when I am talking to you!'

I ignore him, hoping he will go away and have some mercy. Please leave.

But no…

'You are disgusting do you know that, your family upbringing has made you like this, and your fucked up childhood…...'

To speed things up I close my eyes and complete his monologue for him.

'I am a bitch, I am disgusting, my family is disgusting, my sister is a whore, my mother is a bitch, we are from a fucked up background and I am nothing and everyone hates me,' I say.

He looks at me with that death stare and I panic, thinking I may have spoken a bit too much. I put my head down and he stops, (at this point, saying his monologue usually saves me half an hour to hour or mores worth of abuse. My public acknowledgement of his views would save me from the relentless ranting on some occasions). I keep looking down as I can see his shoes and know he is still there.

What is he waiting for?

Is he going to start again?

Why has he not fucked off yet.

'Look at me,' he repeats, 'I don't want to fight, you are my best friend. I forgive you, let's move forward…'

Here we go again. Let's move on. He FORGIVES ME…

I keep my head down and count to five under my breath to allow him time to get out of my room before I run to lock the door this time.

And breathe.

*

My biggest regret is that my children also endured the abuse, but I needed time to build enough emotional strength and gain financial independence to free myself from it. During this time, they used to try saving me from the abusive outbursts. What they witnessed should have been safeguarded. I've since learnt that this act of protection (hiding us away from the abusive outbursts) is judged as parental alienation by the courts (based on this finding, perhaps I should instead have let the children continue hearing and witnessing abuse instead of trying to protect them even though children exposed to abuse is also supposed to be against the Domestic Abuse Act 2021 - Section 3!).

Neither myself nor my children were afforded any such protection, instead I was punished for it.

"Overall, I found his evidence straightforward. He accepted that he had been guilty of loss of patience and anger and shouting, though probably I think not the extent of it. Indeed, he could hardly assert otherwise. There is contemporary evidence to support the contention that the father also shouted at the children. At the very least they were clearly caught in crossfire between their parents, and it is more likely than not that that at least they felt they were being shouted at by their father, and irrespective of its truth the children felt unsafe because of their parents behaviours (for the avoidance of doubt I put the allegation of X being denied the toilet in this category. I accept the father's evidence about this)."

"I accept that there were altercations, not just verbally but scuffles between the parents, and albeit that this was X years ago, the children and X in particular are still disturbed even possibly traumatised and undermined by the reminder of those events, leading as they did of course, to the separation of the parents and the ultimate exclusion of the father ; X in particular has an anxiety about the welfare of his mother, whom he loves deeply and who after all has been his primary carer."

UK High Court Judge – Family Division, 2021. Parental Alienation ruling against the mother.

"Protective mothers are placed in an invidious position, in which insisting on presenting evidence of domestic violence or child abuse may be seen as attempts to alienate children from the other parent, which could result in the loss of primary care or contact with their children."

UN Report – Custody, violence against women and violence against children Report of the Special Rapporteur on violence against women and girls, its causes and consequences. April 2023.

24

Lawyering Up

Six Years Ago

Enough was enough. I had to take some positive steps to get out of our toxic relationship, so I asked a friend for some advice – knowing I would be navigating a foreign minefield of divorce under Sharia Law given Prince Harming was Muslim and would therefore fall under the Sharia system.

Having booked an appointment with a highly recommended lawyer, I nervously went along to the meeting after asking the housekeeper, Fiona, to pick up our kids from school, which I usually did. I parked my car in my usual office car park so I could get a taxi to the lawyer because I didn't know the area of her office well.

When I met her, she said, 'I've heard of you.' I was quite well-known through my work and written articles. Oh God, was he going to find out? Alarm bells sounded in my head, but I also knew she was a professional and shouldn't be telling anyone (I hoped).

I explained why I wanted a divorce, and she then asked me a series of questions.

'Do you have an Islamic certificate?'

'Yes.'

'Do you have this...?'

'Yes.'

'Do you have that...?'

'No.'

'Are you ready to proceed today or do you want to go away and think about it?'

Everything about applying for divorce was terrifying, so I opted to think about it. A tiny voice inside me wondered if things could get better. Also, as strange as it may sound, I still wasn't sure I would actually go through with a divorce because I was frightened. Anything could happen; I could lose the children – as Prince Harming had warned me before. What would my family think? Where would we go? What would a divorce in a foreign country be like?

'How much will a divorce cost?' I then asked.

'15,000 dollars for the initial divorce and additional fees for any appeals' she said, and her words hit me like a bullet. I was being drip fed much less than that a month and that was barely enough for my monthly expenditure, kids expenses and household bills. And we know already that I couldn't get any more money.

Even if I was able to gather the money for the divorce, I also had to get my Islamic marriage certificate certified. Those two elements were complex enough but more confusing was the reasons permitted for a woman to apply for divorce under Sharia: Let's keep things simple; he wouldn't need any reason to file divorce against me, but I needed to be able to show 'harm', such as abandonment in marital relations and/or abandonment in fiscal responsibility to the spouse/ the family. I didn't really know what either meant at that stage except that divorce would only be granted to me, as a woman, if I proved 'harm'.

I left the lawyer's office with a lot to consider…

*

On my way home, Prince Harming telephoned me and said, 'Hello, are you alright?'

'Yes, thank you,' I said, wondering if he had eyes everywhere…

'Where are you?' he asked, predictably.

I paused for a minute not knowing what to say. *My God is he watching where I go?* I told him I had gone to the doctor, and he then said, 'OK, I ask because my friend saw your car parked in the office and Fiona said she picked up the kids today.'

What I didn't clock onto until later was that I was using his old iPhone which he gifted to me, rather unusually, and I could not disable the Find My iPhone application… I needed to buy a new phone but I would need time to save money for that, too!

I needed to be careful from now on because he clearly had eyes on everything. I, meanwhile, was completely isolated and unable to trust anyone, petrified Prince Harming may find out I was thinking about a divorce. His threats about his rights as a Muslim man in a Muslim country echoed on in my head.

25

Saving Money for a Divorce

I searched high and low to find someone I trusted to get our Islamic marriage certificate attested and eventually found someone to send it off to the relevant Embassy in the UK.

One job complete, but it had taken about two months. I had started running the one hundred metre hurdles but stopped at the second hurdle: to find some way to pay for the divorce without Prince Harming knowing.

I then found some extra work I could do separately before telling Prince Harming that I was going to consult separately from time to time.

'You can't do that. Everything has to be done through the joint business,' he said. Of course he did.

I agreed and did some other freelance work that got paid into the business account so he could see some money coming in from those other jobs. And guess what, I had to issue an invoice to my own company to get the extra commission for the freelance work I was being paid for into the business account. I didn't care by this stage because my plan was coming to fruition. I was edging closer to being able to employ the divorce lawyer.

I watched my bank balance grow towards that golden target

of 15,000 dollars- and my hope grew once again- I could see light at the end of the tunnel- or at least a dim light of hope- but hope nonetheless

Eight months later, I had actually saved a lot more and was finally seeing the fruits of earning all that I worked for. Keeping one step ahead of the game, I bought a cash passport from a money transfer bureau (a common product used by the huge expat community in the Middle East) and saved my earnings. That way, I had started building a nest egg for when the children and I were eventually free of our captor. If we were ever going to be...

In the meantime, I told my parents what was going on and was relieved to hear that they were horrified by the position I found myself in and told me they would support me in any decision. That offered some light relief.

*

It was astounding that the above act of saving for months to free myself was also punished by the family justice system- clearly an abused woman should not plan to escape - for such planning is seen negatively, pre-meditated and not how an abused woman is expected to behave - yet no-one in the family justice system has been able to explain how an abused woman with no funds, no emotional strength, no records of her own, no independent visa status, no independent bank access is supposed to make her way out of the abuse discreetly, whilst still living with the abuser until she reaches an appropriate point or legal process of safety nor understand that this can take months or years!

26

Happy Birthday to Me

Autumn Six Years Ago

My birthday. I wake up to a message from my sister reading: 'Dad has been found unresponsive by paramedics. On the way to the hospital.'

I drag myself downstairs in floods of tears, and You Know Who follows me down while continuing some argument he had conjured up the night before. He can see I am crying and yet he won't stop. I am numb. I run into the kitchen. He follows me into the kitchen and attempts to close the door.

Thankfully, my four and six-year-old kids creep into the kitchen using Coping Mechanism Number Six and his barrage stops only when they start singing and giggling loudly whilst running around shooting play guns and then ask me to come into the other room for my surprise... showing me that they have set up a little area for my birthday in the living room. They had also released me from the dreaded 'lock her in a room and shout at her routine'.

There is a balloon and bowl of crisps on the table. To top it off, they give me one of their toys wrapped up in a piece of paper. It's such a sweet thought from my two little saviours.

Prince Harming follows me into the room to say, 'Right, I'll forgive you, let's move forward and go out for your birthday.'

FORGIVE ME?!

There is it is again, abuse, intimidate and then forgiveness, all in one day!

Coping Mechanism Number Six: Distract him.

I don't control this one. My children hear him shouting at me and distract him by putting things in his pockets like hangers attached to his belt or play-shoot guns around him. This causes him to be distracted, which gives me enough time to get out of the room and into another to lock the door. It's a shame that part of their childhood has been spent having to do that…

We go to a cafe and sit in silence because the kids are clearly petrified. I am still numb. The tables are tightly spaced with other customers filling up the cafe. He is sitting on his high horse as if nothing has happened. My children and I sit in silence, terrified of saying or doing anything wrong. Prince Harming starts his ranting again because we were not speaking to him or not 'moving forward' (the usual complaint). He starts his loud 'lecture', but, thankfully, a man in the table behind us turns round and tells Prince Harming that he does not want to listen to a 'domestic' and to keep it down! Thankfully, although he is clearly agitated and enraged by the comment, he shuts up, and as usual called for the bill to cut our lunch short.

You're probably wondering why the hell I hadn't gone back to my lawyer now that I had the money for the divorce.

It's really difficult to explain, (I tried to in Chapter 20.) All I can say is that I was emotionally exhausted and terrified of pulling the trigger on the divorce. Perhaps his voice was in my head, from when he had once said, 'You can never divorce me under Sharia Law, and everything, including the kids, will come to me if you ever tried.'

I was scared.

Was he right? The lawyer certainly hadn't painted a rosy picture of the process... and I was physically and mentally exhausted and petrified that once I pull the trigger, if I am not granted my divorce and sent back to him, he will have carte blanch to do whatever he wants. There is only one chance to get out... only the victim/ survivor of domestic abuse understands that... it takes huge courage to take that first step and we need to be 1000% sure we will make it out... *and stay out.*

*

I travelled to the UK a few days after with the children to see my Dad- my Dad was always a dominant strong man, here he lay in hospital having suffered an acute stroke.

He couldn't speak or move.

I looked at him thinking, 'I am this man's daughter and I deserve better than I have.'

Enough was enough.

To hell with it, I had to get out of that never-ending black hole, not quite knowing the consequences or how I was going to do it - but I had to do it! From that point onwards I would use his anger, his abuse to fuel my focus to get away from him.

27

Filing for Divorce

When I returned, I finally plucked up the courage and engaged the divorce lawyer and she set up an appointment for me to go to the courts to see a Family Counsellor, which was the first stage of filing for a divorce. The ball was rolling. My lawyer then sent me to the Sharia Court, which was nerve-wracking in itself. There, I had to prove my case of 'harm', explaining the abandonment by my husband. The court designated family counsellor asked for Prince Harming's telephone number so he could notify him that I was filing for divorce and that the process had officially begun.

My legs fell further into an abyss, thinking about what would happen when he found out, or worse, what he would do to me if I failed in getting a divorce… I had to go home to him while this process was in motion!

The court family counsellor dialled his number.

He didn't answer.

He rang again.

He didn't answer.

He rang a final time.

He didn't answer.

Our time in court was over with no response from Prince Harming. I had to go home wondering what I would say, or when he may return the court's call.

*

I opened the front door to see Prince Harming's cousin had turned up without any prior notice. Nothing was said about the phone calls, so I didn't know if the court had finally got through to Prince Harming. I was, of course, too scared to ask. I was told by his cousin that every marriage has difficulties, and we should not give up. I did not know if the court had finally got through, did they know, were they messing with me. I was petrified and nodded and stayed quiet.

Prince Harming travelled back to Latin America the following day and I was not aware of his return details because only Fiona, the housekeeper, was privy to that information and I was not allowed to ask about his whereabouts without me facing another barrage of abuse.

I was called back to court.

After explaining my case, the family counsellor passed the divorce papers to the judge, so all wheels were in motion for getting a divorce in a foreign country. The fear of remaining married to this man was far worse than pursuing a divorce in an unknown process, under Sharia, in a foreign country.

I was taking a leap of faith. Only God could help and protect me now.

Around this time, I also obtained assistance to gain access to a senior contact at the bank that held our joint business account and filed some papers to regain some access to my own financial information, this was achieved only after very senior involvement, a call to the regulator, the embassy, and numerous others - all to gain access to my own financial records!

Then, I received Prince Harming's call.

'I'm not going to get angry with you, but I'm just going to ask you why you have removed me?' Prince Harming asked.

My lawyer had already prepared me and told me not to discuss anything with him, so I told him I wouldn't talk about it before saying, 'I have filed for divorce.' I then hung up the phone, petrified.

He was in town at the time, so I dreaded going home to face him. Things then got worse when I learned that his cousin, who was in the UK at the time, was also flying into town to talk with both of us. His cousin's sense of urgency about the divorce was unnerving.

That evening, Prince Harming and his cousin were very business-like.

'OK, you've decided about a divorce and that's fine, but we need to make these arrangements properly and don't need to go to the courts to do that,' they said, even though the divorce was already in process. I was pushed, cajoled and bullied over the next few days until they set out their expectations, the key element being that I would not take any financial settlement or alimony for the children anywhere in the world. I could have sole custody of the children in return, but I could not poke around into financial records.

Isn't it amazing how all those years of marriage had come down to him not even once questioning the divorce but only what he would get out of it?

My cousin-in-law wanted to be in town until it was all signed through the relevant legal process, but, having waited a few days, he had to go home. It still needed to be formally agreed, executed in English and Arabic and then accepted and presented in court.

I then heard from my lawyer.

I was told to stay calm and avoid being left alone with Prince Harming during the process. He was travelling and I had no idea when or where he would return from and waited for the next step. The next step would be going to court for divorce hearings before the judge.

28

Gaining Some Financial Access

With lots of senior assistance, I finally gained signatory status to request financial information over the joint business account and took that certificate into the bank, flying high in anticipation that they would finally deal with ME and not telephone Prince Harming every time I wanted to look into our accounts. All I wanted was copies of all bank statements – as I still had no access to the almost non-existent funds in the account.

I hit a brick wall, however, being sent from pillar to post to attempt obtaining access to my own financial records, from country head of the global bank in question to the local financial regulator. Finally, I was referred to the head of compliance at the bank, but it took a further ten months to be given my records via six or more branches unrelated to where the account was held! And, whilst I eventually got some more information, several months later, I was still chasing the remaining ones. The fact that there were so many obstructions in gaining access to my own financial records, and over ten months to access information, is something that remains an open issue with the relevant institution, which is a global bank and signatory to the UK Finance Abuse codes and runs marketing campaigns against economic abuse!

Reading the accounts and statements made everything clear,

I had no control, no access rights, no ability to take or transfer money from the main account - all set up with the initial documentation coordinated by Prince Harming, at the outset all those years ago, and I was unaware. I was, meanwhile, kept in overdraft for over eight years.

29

Divorce Proceedings

Following the initiation of the divorce process and referral to court, the divorce hearing before the judge began and Prince Harming didn't turn up. Worse still, he filed a submission stating, *'This person filing for divorce is not my wife. My wife's name is Alia* (my Islamic name).' I had filed using my legal name as stated on all my documents, including my passport as I did not have any documents under my Islamic name, except on my Islamic marriage certificate, and only he knew that! This is when I realised how dirty and harmful he was going to be. My heart sank as I stood in the midst of Sharia proceedings in an Islamic country – all at the mercy of a Muslim man who has just denied knowing me.

Fortunately, the judge ignored him entirely, perhaps wandering whether not knowing me meant that he could not possibly know my children? Perhaps that is why the judge refused contact rights to the children in the final divorce judgement; Prince Harming never asked for access to his own children but *did* ask for financial compensation from – which the judge denied. (Looking back, the Middle East judges showed some empathy or understanding, or perhaps frustration at the tactics being played.)

As part of the proceedings, we were referred to two Sharia scholars. During the meeting with the Sharia Scholars, I met with the Sharia scholars first and answered their questions. I was then taken to a separate room to wait while Prince Harming was brought into the room to have his say and they asked him questions to prove he had abandoned me, which he acknowledged himself, also pleading no financial resources and abandonment of fiscal responsibility[16,17]. I was brought back into the room but still didn't really know what was going on, but I then signed something, as did Prince Harming, and we were asked to leave the court.

The Sharia scholars were kind, asking me to wait whilst Prince Harming went down first. Then, they accompanied me down, aware that I was scared to be alone with Prince Harming, especially after these submissions. As we waited for a taxi, they saw Prince Harming drive past in his sports car. Less than thirty minutes prior he had pleaded poverty to the same Sharia scholars! The Sharia scholars were compassionate and told me that I could contact them if there was any problem during the divorce process. It provided some comfort navigating this unknown process. They released their report and Prince Harming submitted a response indicating that their findings and that my claim for a divorce was wrong. He, apparently, was the victim and would now like to file for a divorce. This submission was rejected, and after all of the trials and tribulations, the judge granted my divorce, ruling in my favour! It had been four months, relatively quick in the grand scheme of things. I was, supposedly, a free woman. I was granted my divorce on the grounds of 'harm', with no contact rights given to Prince Harming for the children. Alimony payments for the children including housing allowance (a figure slightly lower than his share of the mortgage), as no alimony is required to be paid to the mother post-divorce.

And breathe – or so I thought.

30

Still More…

As part of the divorce process, an appeal process exists to challenge aspects of the divorce, and most specifically, the alimony order. On day twenty-nine of the thirty day appeal window, Prince Harming appealed the terms of the divorce and continued the flurry of legal proceedings.

A few months after the divorce is granted, Prince Harming then files a travel ban on the children, a notification being emailed to me via the digital court system. After which, Prince Harming left for Latin America and London for four to five months where he was visiting his girlfriend – now wife. Great pictures of them on London Bridge were posted across Facebook! Whilst the children were subject of the travel ban which meant my children could not leave the country until the appeal process was over, or longer.

I was devastated.

From that point on, permission to travel with the children was either granted through permission from their father (unlikely!) or by approaching a judge to ask for his permission. To do that, I had to have a valid reason such as medical reasons. I couldn't just ask to go on holiday. And I didn't trust Prince Harming, of course, being a man who had denied knowing me in court.

So, I always went to the court to ask the judge for permission, who would then contact Prince Harming. If he didn't respond after a couple of days, which he didn't, it was then the judge's responsibility to make sure I wasn't a flight risk. So, the judge would issue a demand for someone to act as a guarantor by giving their passport to the court. After which, a travel permit would be given and upon our return the guarantor would be able to retrieve his or her passport. The court would then issue a copy of the order via the digital court system to Prince Harming.

First, I had been trapped in a marriage and now I was trapped in the Middle East with my children. Plus, my daughter was suffering from a bad bout of eczema that caused her skin to bleed, particularly when temperatures hit over fifty degrees (as was common in the Middle Eastern summer). I wanted to leave to a better climate, but I wasn't allowed. My poor, poor girl.

Meanwhile, Prince Harming was travelling back and forth across the globe.

31

The Appeal

Five Years Ago

Now that Prince Harming had appealed the court ruling, my troubles were not over. In fact, naively, they had only just begun.

He had specifically appealed the financial settlement for the children and we also became embroiled in a custody battle. I can't remember how many times I had to re-apply for the custody of my children, as Prince Harming would submit a custody application every so often to frustrate the court process and intimidate me and delay the finalisation of the court process – resulting in my custody of the children being suspended along with suspension of financial payments to the children. A mothers worst fear is losing her children - an abuser's greatest weapon is that fear and control that can be wielded through the courts.

During these appeals, however, the court released Prince Harming's travel and other documents, such as his bank accounts – yes plural – he had over six accounts across four or five banks, all of which I knew nothing about. I learned that he had a number linked to his cousin's Middle East bank accounts, even though his cousin was based in the UK. There was also a family tax consultant with linked Middle East bank accounts.

This was all very confusing; money seemed to be going round in circles and the bank seemed to be ignorant to it. There was a web of accounts linked to each other so Prince Harming, his cousin and his cousin's tax consultant could move money around through property purchases, property to cash, cash into cars and then back into cash. Round and round it went like a washing machine, making my head spin as I was asked to sift through all the court documents and provide a summary to my lawyers.

I was in total shock.

In the meantime, Prince Harming just kept filing applications to keep the court process moving, meaning he could withhold payments, divert payments from joint accounts and control the finances[18,19].

My biggest worry, however, was whether or not I would have my kids with each application having the potential to impact the custody of my children.

Long story short, there was mercy in the Middle East court, or perhaps the judge was frustrated with the games Prince Harming kept playing. In most submissions, Prince Harming blamed the judge, the previous court, the Sharia scholars, the family counsellor; everyone except himself! Whichever it was, the judge was so annoyed with Prince Harming 'baseless' submissions, as they called them, that, almost three years after the beginning of the divorce process, they issued the final judgement. Thankfully, this made it clear to Prince Harming that he wasn't paying towards the joint mortgage for my benefit, but for his own children. This being in response to Prince Harming filing a submission that he was losing potential financial use of his share of the house because I was living in my share of the house and also using his half of the house!

The child support went up. The housing allowance went up. Everything went up.

Most importantly for me, I had custody of my children (again).

32

Travel Bans

During the never-ending court process, I was going from doctor to doctor to get advice on my daughter's eczema. She had frequent skin infections, was put on antibiotics regularly, and was in and out of hospital. She was bullied for her appearance and other kids would not sit with her at school nor invite her to birthday parties. It was awful.

She still covers her arms and legs to stop her eczema being visible. Even though now her skin is very well under control and she no longer has the same degree of visible outbreaks on her skin, thanks to the medicated creams her UK paediatric dermatologist had prescribed, only time will release her trauma.

Meanwhile, Prince Harming was frequently travelling in and out of town at a time when he didn't have contact rights; if you recall because he did not ask for contact and had denied even knowing me to the judge in the first court.

To fight this, with separate proceedings regarding the children running since for three years, he had started a barrage of attacks on me and my children. He used nannies to say things that simply weren't true. According to him, I wasn't bathing them or buying them new clothes. So, I had to counter by getting the school to confirm that these were all lies. I had to counter everything he had conjured up. Deflection is his superpower – he would send me on a wild goose chase to defend myself from one of his lies and avoid facing any personal criticism of his own.

Open Jail?

Whilst Prince Harming was increasing his attacks, he was submitting various allegations against me to the court in the child contact case. But when all else was failing, he had a hidden gem up his sleeve – religion! Prince Harming told the court, in the contact hearing, that I left our children with non-Muslim family members, my mother and sister. So, an order was issued by the court of appeal that determined that the children must remain in the Middle East if ever I travelled.

I couldn't believe it.

I scurried around from lawyer to lawyer trying to understand what that meant until one lawyer bluntly stated: 'Your children cannot leave the Middle East until they are eighteen and like many other mothers you are stuck here with your children until then, unless you leave without them.'

And that was it, I was trapped indefinitely. It was that simple for him to do, with the consequences felt by the children. Meanwhile, Prince Harming's travels continued during that time when the appeal court had just laid down in judgement that we had no way out. The children couldn't leave the country with me under any circumstances; there was no going to the judge to seek permission to travel, not even with a guarantor.

We were, again, in an open jail.

And the only reason for any of this was that Prince Harming knew that alimony would be paused while that appeal process was underway.

Words cannot justify the anguish. My stories cannot describe the pain. Quite frankly, it's a wonder that I am still alive or sane. Yet, it is well noted that women are usually labelled mad, sad or bad in family proceedings, regardless of what the abuser seems to do or has done to them!

It was exhausting.

I was trapped... *again.*

My world collapsed from underneath me, and that all too familiar feeling of being trapped with no way out and wanting to scream when no one could hear me washed over me. I felt dead – with my two tiny children trapped in the Middle East because of their devout, alcohol-drinking, partying Muslim father playing the religion card in a Sharia process!

I contacted the British Embassy and Reunite to let them know what had happened. They couldn't do anything other than the British Embassy giving me a letter that confirmed I was a British National, which I took with me from court to court. Reunite did, however, remain in touch for more than two years, calling in regularly to check if we were OK.

Just when I thought court days were over, I now had to appoint another lawyer, this time one who had the right to represent in the highest court of the land, the Supreme Court. The final court. The final decision.

My case was looked at by some senior lawyers and they thought it looked like a total mess – being baffled that a mother couldn't travel with her children even though the law permits it – and a hearing was finally set after a lot of back and forth on a point of law.

My lawyers had told me that I didn't need to attend the

hearing as they had made the submissions directly to the court – but something within me told me I should go.

Thank God I did!

33

The Final Decision

I was waiting outside the courtroom. The hearing was about to start, time was ticking by and my lawyer still hadn't arrived, so I turned to a security guard and asked him to help me. As I couldn't find my lawyer, the compassionate security guard let me into the courtroom. I could not let this last chance for my children slip by.

I was shaking when walking through the humungous floor to ceiling double doors into a large room. Five judges were sitting on a raised podium looking down at me when the security guard explained that my lawyer hadn't arrived and that I wanted to sit in on the hearing. The judge agreed before asking if I needed a translator. Then, another judge said he could translate on my behalf, so we were underway. It was extremely unnerving, and I had no idea what was going on.

'You can speak now,' one of the judges said.

I stood to talk but I was trembling through my tears and could hardly get a word out. I was petrified, my children's freedom resting on what comes out of my mouth... What if I failed them? There is no other court after this one, this decision was final. I trembled from head to toe, tears streaming down my face and nothing but mumbling rolling from my lips.

'OK Miss, calm down, and breathe,' one of the judges said.

I didn't know what to say, or how the hearing was meant to be conducted, so I held up a blown-up picture of my tiny daughter smiling, with her front teeth missing and her peeling face and bleeding skin, while saying, 'The father travels freely and my children cannot. Please let my children go. Just let us go. I don't want anything else, please let us go.'

I didn't know what I was supposed to be asking for or how the hearing was to be conducted because my lawyers had, apparently, submitted everything to the court on my behalf. So, I just took the opportunity to plead. I was desperate, begging, and tears kept streaming down my face. I don't even know if the judges heard me.

'Please let me and my children go. Please,' I begged.

The judges appeared shocked by the picture I was holding up. They were fleetingly speechless. I stood there in tears holding the photograph of my daughter high above my head; her tiny smiling face covered in peeling infected skin from her eczema.

'Do you have cream?' one of the judges asked.

'I have cream, I have doctors, we have gone to the hospital,' I replied.

'Where is the father?'

'We don't know.'

'OK. You can go now.'

I was in there for maybe ten minutes. But it was ten minutes that I will never forget.

The following January, the court of appeal travel prohibition was overturned by the supreme court – stating that 'It is the right of the children to travel with their mother.'

And breathe.

Now, I was only subject to Prince Harming's travel ban, and once again had the right to approach a judge for permission to leave the country. I wanted to get the hell out of there on the first chance I got, but I was scared; I had just started a new business – my only means of looking after my children – and I didn't have a home or life in England.

Where should I go? Where was home?

I was still SO confused, scared and on eggshells because I didn't know what Prince Harming would throw at me next, or when he would do it, but I had no choice but to keep going one day at a time. I told myself to keep putting one foot in front of the other and to keep moving. Don't look back – just keep moving.

34

Travelling Again

Shortly after the travel judgement, I sought permission to travel to the UK as my Dad was hospitalised again. To apply, I needed a medical note explaining why I was leaving, confirmation of medical treatment for my daughter, evidence of a return ticket and a guarantor who would be willing to leave their passport with the judge as collateral against my risk of flight…

Nine days were granted, and I could finally tie my trip to the UK in with seeking further medical advice on my daughter's skin condition. The children were over the moon to be able to go on an airplane again.

We stayed with my parents who were relieved to see us, even if only permitted for a few days. They had provided all the medical records for my father that were needed to be submitted with the travel request to the courts. Our little bit of freedom was refreshing before we returned to the Middle East.

That Summer I applied to travel again. By now, the doctors in England had given me medical appointments for my daughter spanning across six weeks to keep her skin managed. As her father didn't give his permission for us to go, despite her skin condition, the judge asked for a guarantor again. Thankfully, a friend who was in a comparable situation to me acted as guarantor and we were on our way. The travel order stipulated that I returned to the Middle East one day after my daughter's birthday, meaning we would have to travel on her birthday to get to court the following morning to submit our documents. In situations like this you don't argue, instead taking what you are given!

*

The kids and I had a great time strawberry picking, visiting farms, enjoying a bit of freedom, relaxing in cooler weather – and just a bit of normality.

Prince Harming, however, sent an SMS two or three days before we left that said he was going to come and pick the kids as we had managed to get to the UK.

'You know we have travelled, the court contacted you to inform you with a copy of the court order that they always send to you,' I replied.

'Nobody told me.'

I ignored him knowing full well that the court would have contacted him and emailed a copy of the order (most of the proceedings were electronic). But he travelled to the UK and insisted on seeing the children the day we were expected to fly back - all of this documented well across his SMS's!

He knew that I had to leave the UK in order to meet the court's deadline, but said I was deliberately refusing. I responded indicating that we had to fly back to comply with the court order and ignored his ranting SMS, and took the children back to the

Middle East not knowing when or how we might be permitted to travel again.

Our little bit of freedom had come to an end.

He was constantly playing games like that. To make matters worse, if that's possible, my cat (a friend for seventeen years) died barely a week after we had returned from the UK that Summer. Prince Harming found out and messaged me saying that he was devastated that I hadn't told him that 'his' cat had died and that he was upset that I had cremated him. Under Islam, cremation was not permitted, but I did not respond to his SMS to avoid any risk of breaching Sharia. He was always trying his best to show that I wasn't living the life of a good Muslim, knowing that the Middle East applicable family law made clear that a condition of custody is that the mother has the same religion as the children and that the children are deemed to follow the same religion as the father, in this case Islam.

One false move on my part could jeopardise my custody of my own children… so I was back walking on eggshells.

35

Bricks And Mortar

During the appeal process, Prince Harming had made multiple submissions about the family home with the courts, refusing to pay his share of the mortgage now that he wasn't living in it. I decided to take things into my own hands.

In Summer, after returning from our trip to the UK and now with the final court judgement on the financial settlement in hand, I went to the bank and said, 'Here is the court order determining that my ex-husband is supposed to be paying towards the joint mortgage with me. He's not. Please repossess the house and get it sold.'

The mortgagor told me that the way to do that was to default a certain number of times before the case would be taken to court to begin a repossession order. All I asked was that they didn't put repossession notices on the door, as I didn't want the children to see that.

You may be wondering why I didn't just put the house on the market to sell it, but that would mean getting Prince Harming involved, who would clearly not have agreed unless on his terms. My children's freedom and my peace of mind were far more valuable than the house, so the court could do what they wanted with the house as far as I was concerned.

In the meantime, Prince Harming refused to pay the alimony (which under Sharia is to the children). He even cited that he was not financially stable, as his sports car was under a loan so part of his mounting debts! The judge was not impressed and a warrant was issued to collect three years' worth of back-dated child-support.

Moving On

I completed the required number of months of defaulted mortgage payments, blessed the house on the way out, and cut all ties with that part of my life.

I rented a two-bedroom apartment on the beach front. It felt small compared to our five-bedroom house but it was right on the beach, with a beach club with a kids pool and abundance of chicken nuggets and ice-cream! I was doing my best to keep some form of stability and what my children had become accustomed to.

I then learned that Prince Harming had started paying minimal payments on the house to stop it being repossessed.

Just as I needed his signature to sell the house when I went down the route of defaulting on mortgage payments, he now needed mine to sell it. Whilst the house had gone up considerably in value, I didn't trust him at all. So, I now had the court managing the process. Being saddled with the sole responsibility of the mortgage to keep a roof over my children's heads was used to try to financially harm and continue to control us.

I had to cut that ball and chain, too…

36

Freedom?

Autumn - Four Years Ago

My daughter's skin was so bad that her paediatric dermatologist in London had insisted we needed to be there for a while because he determined that her condition was likely stress related and the medication being prescribed may be too strong for prolonged use. Her father's actions were seeping through to my children. With that, however, came some good news. The doctors in England gave me medical appointments for her that spanned across four months, putting it in writing so I could apply to the court for a travel permit.

Hallelujah, the judge permitted us to travel to the UK for four months on the condition that I returned for one week in January. I went through the same process to arrange a guarantor but something miraculous then happened. The travel permit was issued *before* my guarantor left her passport… I had a travel permit with *no guarantor.* I wondered if it was some sort of test but also thought it might be my ticket to freedom.

I carried on as normal, going to the police station to ensure all the bans were lifted in their systems as part of the usual travel permit process.

They were.

I then went to the airport police to ensure the bans were lifted in their systems.

They were.

I was scared. Trembling. Excited.

'Just get out,' I told myself repeatedly.

I didn't have much to my name now that I had left our big house and most of the items in it, so I packed our suitcases, and even packed my daughter's doll house and told the school I was taking them to London for four months.

Then, I made final preparations to leave the Middle East, not knowing when we would return…

37

Lift Off

On the morning of the flight, we wake up super early because I could not sleep the night before from being petrified about missing my alarm clock – our flight.

I am walking through the airport on autopilot. There are four checkpoints I need to clear, even though I have checked with the police systems over the last three days that all the bans have been removed. Carrying a suitcase in each hand and balancing my daughter's dolls house as well, I must have looked like a travelling circus with all this baggage.

Have you ever had that feeling of wanting something so much and the fear of something going wrong? That's how I felt exiting the airport, not knowing if I could be turned back at any checkpoint, or if I would make it through them all... after going from court to court, dealing with the father's travel ban, a court ban, and then a supreme court over turn... it was a whirlwind and emotional rollercoaster getting to that day.

First, I check in our suitcases and the dolls house – watching as our worldly belongings roll off into the abyss of the airport's mechanics.

Checkpoint one cleared.

Next stop – immigration.

I carry the children's rucksacks as well as my carry-on luggage so that the immigration officer might feel sorry for me being burdened with so much and process us quickly. My hands are full, so I ask my son to look after the passports. We queue up. I'm trembling with fear and excitement but trying to remain poker-faced. We are called forward. My son hands our passports to the immigration officer. The immigration officer takes the passports, scan-reads the various pages, and waves us through.

Another HUGE hurdle completed.

Checkpoint two completed.

I take the kids for pancakes at a café in the airport. I can't eat. I glance down at my phone to see how long it is until we can board the flight. Time seems to be going in reverse. We arrive at the gate and show our tickets and passports to the friendly lady behind a desk as she ushers us through.

Checkpoint three cleared!

But there is yet another security check ahead of us, the one before you enter the final boarding lounge. Thankfully, I still have the kids' rucksacks and my carry-on luggage, so the security man waves us through without stopping us.

Checkpoint four cleared!

Relief streams off my back as we sit down at the gate, the only thing separating the torment and our freedom being a one hundred metre jet bridge.

'We would like to begin boarding all passengers with children under ten years old,' the Tanoy announcement is music to my ears.

I shoot up. Hurry to the front of the queue. Ferry my children onto the plane. I feel like a lifetime passes by as we sit and wait for boarding to be completed. The ground staff shortly leave the plane…the door is secured and everyone is told to sit down and buckle up…nearly there!. The plane's engines whir into action and we are eventually taxiing to the runway. I sit patiently.

The plane accelerates down the runway.

We lift off.

Tears stream down my face with the biggest exhale I have mustered in months.

And I breathe.

Touching down in Heathrow seven hours later is the first time I am ever happy to be in grey, wet, blustery, England.

We have made it.

38

Lockdown to Freedom

I had only been in the UK for two weeks before Prince Harming started his barrage of threats and abuse – questioning why I was in the UK with our children without his permission. I knew full well that this was his usual drama, caused whenever the court contacted him for consent to travel, releasing copies of the travel orders via their digital court system. We focussed on enjoying the UK while he ranted on in the background.

*

Weeks before we were due to travel back to the Middle East, the British Prime Minister, Boris Johnson, told the country that we were going into lockdown. The infamous Covid-19 virus was running rife in the UK. The world was in shock, but I shouted, 'I bloody love you Boris!' at the television screen.

The Middle East, like so many other countries, also closed its borders.

God was looking down on me after all. The world had locked down, making it impossible for us to return.

39

September

One day before my birthday, Prince Harming notifies me of yet another court application, this time via the UK courts. He also added claims of abuse to him as part of his contact arrangements request a process that I now understand to be DARVO (Deny, Attack, Reverse, Victim, and Offender) - a process he did in the Middle East courts too, blaming everyone else for everything.

> "Research has shown that often perpetrators of domestic abuse, when facing allegations of abuse, will deny these allegations and attack the victim and survivor to make professionals question the victim or survivor's credibility. They will then reverse the status of perpetrator and victim or survivor to secure their own position as a victim and position the person who has been a victim of their abuse as the perpetrator. This is known as DARVO: Deny, Attack, Reverse, Victim, and Offender)."[20]
>
> *Domestic Abuse Commissioner – The Family Court and domestic abuse: achieving cultural change. July 2023.*

On our arrival back to the UK, I had hidden my location until Prince Harming's solicitors, through some form of legal submission, tracked me down. Isn't it great to know you are not safe or secure anywhere! The relevant agency disclosed my county to his solicitors. It is also worth noting that it is common practice for Prince Harming to do something to me around special occasions, special dates to intimidate, add stress – or just be vindictive – a pattern that has continued. Believe it or not, his lawyers even sent me a lovely legal letter one day before the removal of my second lump in 2023 after being notified of the forthcoming surgery dates.

The court hearing started in a local court, then ended up in the High Court due to the international element. The judge agreed to keep my exact location confidential until the case progressed. At this first hearing, Prince Harming discloses to the court that he has remarried but it is a special occasion, so he will speak to the children to let them know when the time is right. Noting that the date of marriage was disclosed as September 2019, and recall that we left in November 2019. In true coercive and manipulative style, the fact that the children had not been informed was again somehow my fault... accused as part of his defence, of removing the children from the Middle East preventing the disclosure of the new step-mother.

If I add the time scales up correctly, September is two months before November and that is when Prince Harming was having contact with the children... If I consider this further, if you are planning to remarry you would plan a few months before and would want to engage your children, surely? Or let us go back to the default position: blame the mother for anything.

At the time of publication of this book, Prince Harming *still* hasn't disclosed the existence of the children's new stepmother. Clearly there is a different rule for fathers.

Part 3

The Family Justice System

40

Prove It

The outcome I was hoping for through the courts was to make any contact arrangements safe for me and my children. I hoped I would have stability in a stressful enough process. That is not what happened. I did not anticipate that I would be forced into contact with Prince Harming. I was not aware of the problems in the system and I had no idea what was coming.

> "The secrecy around the Family Court creates a lot of trauma. Women go into the process thinking that they are going to get justice and their abuse will be acknowledged, but that is not what the Family Court can offer."
>
> *Domestic Abuse Commissioner's roundtable discussion on the Family Court (September 2021)*

> "What astounds me is that the same court that grants a non-molestation order and says this person is not safe to be around you, is the same court that says this person is safe to be around your children. You are told to leave an abusive relationship but when you do, you are very definitely penalised for it by the Family Court system."
>
> *Correspondence to Domestic Abuse Commissioner*

As in any court, credible evidence is needed to support a claim, especially of abuse, but that is much harder when it is non-physical abuse. Even the physical abuse I experienced was undermined and disregarded as historical because I had no police report, even though I had evidence of communications with RELATE; and even Prince Harming implicitly acknowledged it. It seems non-physical domestic abuse evidence can be contested and, argued well, dismissed. I was stunned when I was told that my evidence was *not clear* and that it was not enough, but then in the same hearing, was told I had *too much evidence*; which suggested it was contrived; and counter-argued that I planned everything. It was suggested that I had actually tried to provoke Prince Harming to cause his abusive outbursts. Unfortunately, other women who have also experienced both physical and non-physical abuse with clear evidence have found their position still being undermined, disregarded or simply ignored. So, when women *don't* have enough evidence, they are disadvantaged, when women *do* have evidence, including police and medical evidence, they are still disadvantaged.

'In the case of GK v PR - A fact-finding hearing took place over a year after PR initially filed for the order, taking place in January 2021. GK made twenty-nine separate allegations of domestic abuse, including sexual abuse, verbal abuse and coercive and controlling behaviour. The hearing bundle consisted of over 1000 pages, with the judge having little time to read it before the hearing. The proceedings were conducted on a hybrid basis (i.e. with most of the people involved in the case in court, but with GK joining over video link because she was shielding). GK struggled with the stress of proceedings and was hospitalised after the first day of the hearing. She joined the hearing from the hospital the next day. The judge in the lower court dismissed most of the allegations of domestic abuse which GK had made. He made an order reinstating contact between PR and the child, as well as allowing for overnight contact.'

The case was therefore referred back to the lower court to be re-heard. We note that the appeal judge made clear that his judgment should not be taken as suggesting that GK's allegations are proved.'

Appendix B- The Family Court and domestic abuse: achieving cultural change. The Domestic Abuse Commissioner's second report on the Family Court and domestic abuse.

'... overturn of a fact-finding decision in which no findings were made on the mother's allegations of rape, domestic abuse and coercive and controlling behaviour. The appellate court held that the trial judge minimised the significance of the allegations of abuse, for example, allegations that the father called the mother dirty, fat, fucking stupid, fucking die... were regarded by the judge as stuff of many a "matrimonial row" (§40). The appellate court also highlighted that the family court does not need to find "intentional misconduct" for a finding of abusive behaviour to be made (§40). The appellate court also held that there is a duty on the court to ensure that there are special measures in place to assist a vulnerable witness to give her best evidence. In this case, a complainant of rape did not have special measures and she could see the father when giving evidence; she was subsequently admitted to hospital because she struggled to breathe; and she attended the remote hearing the following day from her hospital bed.'

Dr. Proudman- Goldsmith Chambers in GK v PR

In my own fact-finding decision, I was told that the abuse was not the worst kind the judge has seen but it appears the reference was to physical abuse. And it seemed that all Prince Harming needed to do was make a tearful and sorrow statement to the court to undermine the evidence that I had presented.

Going to court is intimidating especially when your children are at stake. I felt confused, intimidated and scared by the court process and started desperately researching to understand how the system worked; and what was happening to me. That is when I encountered reports (UK Ministry of Justice 'Harm Report' from 2020 and 2023) that critique the handling of domestic abuse cases. I quickly discovered that my experience of courts was not isolated and that it seemed to be the common experience of many domestically abused women. Especially, those who encountered non-physical abuse.

Whilst it was at least comforting to know that I was not alone in my experience it was however, disconcerting to read that despite these anomalies being formally raised, little had changed in the last few years since the issues were highlighted.

As I am still in the court process, I vigilantly monitor new cases, and new reports to find some hope in how to navigate the system and what I should expect in the legal process. It seems that telling the truth, and presenting evidence does not seem to be enough.

> 'Mothers' submissions to the panel stated that they were questioned about why they had not reported allegations to the police and were either told, or got the strong impression, that they were not believed because they had not made a call to the police. However, even in cases where there was evidence from the police, this was not always considered to be relevant.

The panel was told by several mothers that they had reported incidents to the police but when they tried to introduce this as evidence in the family courts it was dismissed or disregarded.'

UK Ministry of Justice 'Harm Report'[21]

Non-Physical Abuse

This issue seems to focus on how courts treat non-physical domestic abuse. Physical abuse can be documented, corroborated and proven more easily in the courts than what I experienced (even though physical abuse is also undermined in some cases) – sustained emotional and psychological abuse, being physically detained, financial restrictions, etc. That abuse is much harder to corroborate and as I discovered very open to dismissal.

For example, a non-physical domestic abuse case was heard by the magistrates, but the mother said she felt that the court were not interested in the abuse and 'attempted to bat away the issue of abuse because I did not have broken bones or physical bruises to show them.' In her view, the court were 'shockingly and dangerously dismissive of serious concerns of domestic abuse'.

UK Ministry of Justice 'Harm Report' 2020

Promise of Change?

It is encouraging that the UK has highlighted the issues facing women and children in the family justice system, so is change coming since the 2020 Harm Report?[22,23]

In June 2022, Women's Aid issued the following in relation to the Harm Report that the Family courts remain an unsafe and traumatic place for women and children

'Two years after a government report into the family courts, Women's Aid has found the justice system is still failing domestic abuse survivors and their children. In 2020, a Ministry of Justice expert panel, the Harm Panel, published a report revealing that the family court system was seriously failing and creating further harm and trauma for women and children in private law proceedings. The government responded by publishing an implementation plan.

The Women's Aid report launched today, two years, too long: Mapping action on the Harm Panel's findings, reveals that despite some progress, not enough work has been done towards the transformed system that the Harm Panel recommended, and there is evidence of progress stalling, even reversing. Domestic abuse survivors and support workers told Women's Aid that they have continued to be disbelieved, children have continued to be forced into unsafe contact arrangements with abusive parents, and perpetrators have continued to use child arrangement proceedings as a form of post-separation abuse. On top of this, survivors and professionals reported that family court professionals have not been held accountable for their poor decision-making and the trauma it has caused.

Key findings include:

- All of the survivors contributing to our report felt that their children's thoughts, wishes or feelings had not been listened to or acted upon;
- An underlying culture of misogyny, mother-blaming and victim-blaming continues in the family courts;
- Women continue to be accused of "parental alienation"

when they raise valid concerns around domestic abuse and child safety;

- Family court proceedings continue to be trauma-inducing, rather than trauma-aware.

Farah Nazeer, chief executive of Women's Aid, said: 'The current system, based on misogyny, victim-blaming, and a lack of understanding trauma is as tragic as it is unacceptable: we must show women and children that they will be listened to, believed and supported... '

In May 2023, Women's Aid issued the following in relation of the progress of the Harm Report[24]:

'Many of the recommendations updated on in this progress report were brought in through the Domestic Abuse Act 2021. Whilst the ban on cross-examination of survivors by perpetrators and introduction of special measures and barring orders are critical, they are not new and we are concerned that they are not being implemented effectively on the ground. We remain unclear what 'compulsory' training on domestic abuse for judges includes, and in our experience women who allege domestic abuse continue to face discrimination and victim-blaming attitudes when trying to secure safe child contact arrangements for their children.

'In some areas, progress is even being reversed. At the same time as publishing this report, the government is consulting on dangerous proposals to make mediation 'compulsory' in the family courts. If this goes ahead, it will have severe consequences for survivors of domestic abuse, who need the protection that the courts provide.

'We urge the government, judiciary and family court professionals to work together with specialist domestic abuse organisations and survivors to deliver the system wide reform which is still so desperately needed to ensure children are put first in the family courts.'

Women's Aid responds to the Harm Panel progress report - Women's Aid (womensaid.org.uk)[25,26,27,28]

In Summer 2023, the UK Domestic Abuse Commissioner echoed the same concerns[29,30]:

Nicola Jacobs was, reportedly having criticized the family courts' handling of domestic abuse, calling for urgent reforms to a family justice system that she says retraumatizes victims, minimizes abuse, and fails to hear the voice of the child.

The report issued by the Domestic Abuse Commissioner highlighted concerns about unsafe contact orders in private law children's proceedings, in particular when allegations of 'parental alienation' are made. It noted that claims of parental alienation – a term used to describe the unwarranted rejection of a parent by a child because of manipulation by the other parent – as a counter-allegation to claims of domestic abuse are having a 'chilling effect' on the ability of parents to disclose abuse in order to ensure safe contact arrangements for their children. The commissioner said there was a feeling among victims and survivors of abuse that these counter-allegations were taken more seriously than allegations of domestic abuse.

Seems like women like me are still waiting for change. At least we don't feel alone or doubt our experience, even if we are made to.

41

The Fact-Finding Hearing

Three Years Ago

We attend the High Court via remote hearings and lots of statements, emails, and text messages dating back to courtship are read aloud. No one deems them irrelevant to the hearing.

The court hearing proceeds, and whilst Prince Harming is not providing any child support on financial grounds, it seems he can pay for solicitors and barristers in a High Court. No judge or social worker raises this as an issue.

Incredibly, the court deduces that the father is genuine and what he did was mostly OK. Prince Harming can restrict travel deemed necessary for the medical treatment of his daughter's skin condition. He can prevent her from going to the toilet, causing her to hold it until she wets herself. And stabbing a butter knife in a child's bottom is portrayed as 'physical play'. And he can lock and detain their mother in rooms and shout at everyone.

The father has now heard the court's feedback and knows he can do ANYTHING to us, and that nobody will care. This feels like *enabling abuse.* You are on that chessboard, and you have just become the pawn in front of the King who has a carte blanch to abuse you because the court has just enabled him…

"The secrecy around the Family Court creates a lot of trauma. Women go into the process thinking that they are going to get justice and their abuse will be acknowledged, but that is not what the Family Court can offer."

Victim/survivor of domestic abuse who attended the Domestic Abuse Commissioner's roundtable discussion on the Family Court (September 2021)

"A lot of people think that court will be a safe space, but instead they find themselves caught in a minefield which they struggle to navigate.... I think I was punished for raising domestic abuse."

Victim/survivor of domestic abuse who attended the Domestic Abuse Commissioner's roundtable discussion on the Family Court (September 2021)

The word *disbelief* does not quite explain what I'm sitting through in this court room. It is as if everything that has happened is being dismissed as *normal.*

Ah, so this is what feeling *unsafe* means.

This is my current experience of the family justice system and many other women's.

42

The Decision

I am stunned. The Family Court rules against me.

".....The *physical* abuse is not of the worst kind it has to be said, but this is a physical manifestation of the father ensuring that his point of view had to be made and was being made forcibly to the mother."

Yes, you read correctly. The physical abuse was not the worst kind the judge had seen. There is, apparently, a pecking order of grades of abuse; perhaps two slaps are worse than one. I'm not sure how much abuse or violence tips the scale before it is not OK, even though the Domestic Abuse Act 2021 states otherwise!

The judge then added:

"The father's behaviour was far worse during the separation, but pales into insignificance due to the mother's behaviour after..."

So, there I was, accused of *parental alienation.* Parental alienation is defined as: 'when a child's resistance or hostility towards one parent is not justified and is the result of psychological manipulation by the other parent.'

It was counter-claimed that I used to lock myself and my children in a room to isolate us from the father rather than protect against the outbursts of abuse; and that it was pre-meditated because I planned my escape (clearly not presenting as an abused woman should behave). Evidence of the father ranting at me, using the 'f' word one hundred plus times, was filed and the judge acknowledged the father does not let the mother get a word in edgewise but still ruled against me. I learnt the rule very quickly: blame the mother for everything and a slap here and there, or being locked in a room is unlikely to offend a judge.

> "I am sure that there were other awful occasions which the children witnessed and, of course, that very much sits comfortably with the behaviour complained of by the mother of the father detaining her in a locked room, the scrap for the keys, scuffles, and it is consistent too with what mother says, and has repeated on a number of occasions, of the one, but isolated occasion, I think, in X when she had Y on her chest, when the mother was pursued. It is consistent with the father insisting that she look at him when they were arguing."
>
> *UK High Court Judge – Family Division, 2021. Parental Alienation decision against mother. in a fact-finding hearing.*

When women enter the family justice system, most of us have little to no understanding, qualifications or experience to navigate legal proceedings that directly impact our lives, nor may we be aware how flawed and biased it is. The stereotypes are potentially harmful, whilst I studied law a few decades ago, that does not mean that I understand family law that is practised daily by solicitors, nor working in a bank makes you an accountant or financially literate. Yet the expectation is very different.

A woman can't be too smart or is not smart enough... or should know better... or would have or should have known. You can't win!

Many women would have retold their experience multiple times to people who cannot hear them or do not want to hear them, yet continue to battle, simply to make the abuse stop or just to be heard, exhausted by repeating their experience to an audience that cannot or does not want to hear them or being retraumatised in the process.

When you start the process, the first hurdle is that of accepting that you were abused, then when you pass the next hurdle of being able to begin to talk about it without the shame. Then, having passed these first few hurdles, you may then find that your own legal team may discourage you from raising any allegations of domestic abuse because they know it will somehow, adversely impact your case, and they will do their utmost to protect your position by actually trying their best to keep you out of court because they know that court will not protect you and may even retraumatize victims/survivors.

"Legal practitioners felt the Family Court would re-traumatise victims and survivors of domestic abuse. Over four fifths (82 percent) of legal practitioners felt that the Family Court were either likely or very likely to re-traumatise victims and survivors of domestic abuse."

Domestic Abuse Commissioner – The Family Court and domestic abuse: achieving cultural change, July 2023.[31]

In trying to or being advised to steer clear of the courts, this may have the consequence of being pushed to consider and agree to orders outside of court that you may not fully agree with nor understand.

> "Women have reported being advised by their legal representatives not to raise allegations of domestic violence, as it would work against them. Research and submissions, including from Germany and the United Kingdom, demonstrate that women experience considerable pressure from courts and their lawyers to agree to contact arrangements or to attend mediation, in some cases without any assessment of child welfare concerns or obtaining the views of the children."
>
> *UN Report – Custody, violence against women and violence against children Report of the Special Rapporteur on violence against women and girls, its causes and consequences. April 2023.*[32]

Remorse?

If any abuser actually feels some remorse and wants to rectify their behaviour to have a better relationship with both mother and child, the courts may not be a place to encourage that, particularly if the abusive behaviour is not even acknowledged by the court to even offer support and proper training to men who wish to change.

The only winners are the participants in the family justice system, where invoicing and fees are the only constant, regardless of the outcome and impact on families. This is especially the case when there has been a finding of parental alienation; it is almost a free-for-all to charge fees for endless processes that may have little or no positive impact on the family; further discrediting, minimising as historical, undermining and disregarding any allegations of domestic abuse and the mother. It will feel like being thrown back into that all too familiar quicksand and trying desperately to get out.....but this time escaping more than just the abuser.

"A punch will hurt for a day or so, but you can't get rid of the pain and trauma of mental and emotional abuse which you have to relive in court."

Victim/survivor of domestic abuse who attended the Domestic Abuse Commissioner's roundtable discussion on the Family Court (September 2021)

"The tendency to dismiss the history of domestic violence and abuse in custody cases extends to cases where mothers and/or children themselves have brought forward credible allegations of physical or sexual abuse. In several countries, family courts have tended to judge such allegations as deliberate efforts by mothers to manipulate their children and to separate them from their fathers. This supposed effort by a parent alleging abuse is often termed 'parental alienation'."

"The report demonstrates how the discredited and unscientific pseudo-concept of parental alienation is used in family law proceedings by abusers as a tool to continue their abuse and coercion and to undermine and discredit allegations of domestic violence made by mothers who are trying to keep their children safe. It also shows how the standard of the best interest of the child is violated by imposing contact between a child and one or both parents and by prioritizing it, even where there is evidence of domestic violence."

UN Report – Custody, violence against women and violence against children Report of the Special Rapporteur on violence against women and girls, its causes and consequences. April 2023.[33]

The above is why it is so important to try to understand, as much as possible, the legal process that is being applied to you. Slowly taking control back over aspects of decisions being taken for you and your children, you can try to prevent others making life changing decisions that only you and your children feel the impact of – all whilst the fees and invoices keep rolling.

As set out in the UK Ministry of Justice report 'Harm Report' in June 2020, the treatment of victim/survivors in contrast to their perpetrators is best illustrated as follows.

I wish I had all these resources and information before I entered the UK court process, rather than being kept in the dark as to what would happen to us.

43

Lump Number Two

Spring - 1 Year Ago

I had discovered a lump behind my ear and kept monitoring it until it grew visibly larger. I was referred to a specialist who discovered I had a parotid tumour growing through my facial nerve. I had no idea what that was but was told that the location of the tumour could lead to facial paralysis if not removed – quickly and carefully. I was petrified because I had the court process running and I feared that any sign of weakness or vulnerability would be exploited.

April - This Year

After monitoring the lump for a year- I was referred to a very senior and highly experienced specialist who organized MRIs, blood tests. Within a few days, he scheduled me for surgery.

The lead up to the surgery and the 'support' I received from the social workers afterwards was 'astounding,' so much so that I requested that the surgeon help as much as possible to expedite my recovery because I knew I would need to defend myself as soon as I come round!

Prince Harming and two independent social workers had

been engaging in direct conversations since early May, possibly longer, to the exclusion of myself and my son. I only knew this when it was identified by my legal representatives; this was Prince Harming's latest plot to agree contact that suited him and to then dictate the details to us. If we were unable to comply, I would be open to criticism for not giving emotional permission for contact (a term used frequently by social workers especially in findings of parental alienation), even if I was not aware of plans that had been agreed without me.

My solicitors raised their concerns about my exclusion from the process, but our requests were ignored even though it have been several weeks when my solicitors submitted a proposal to Prince Harming's solicitors with an acknowledgement and nothing else received; money that could have been better spent on my children instead of wasted legal fees.

Across the next few weeks, to the run up to and immediately after my surgery no compassion was shown.

The fathers' solicitors were advised of the date of the surgery, and after weeks of no response sent a letter the day immediately before the surgery with their detailed letter of actions they will take.

The social worker, after being advised by my solicitors to stop excluding me and my son from contact discussions and stop siloed discussions with the father, continue to ignore this, with the last communication being sent to me days after my surgery with directions on what had been agreed, again, to my exclusion at a date that I could not comply with, again after being legally requested to communicate only with the solicitors.

You can imagine my reaction. I was in recovery, on heavy medication, vomiting, and unable to stand unaided.

Not only had they ignored the solicitor's written email to both social workers, both Prince Harming and the social worker had continued their silo discussions to my exclusion. All done immediately prior to my surgery and immediately after – perhaps I could be forgiven for imagining that it was well-timed. This wasn't only affecting me, but my son had to witness this, all while being the one who was aiding me standing up and supporting me walking after surgery. Perhaps a judge would condone this? – it was for the first lump, why not on the second…

"For example, a matter of some significance to the mother is, she says, the father's callousness to her when a lump was found in her breast or when X had a febrile seizure in X. Illustrations, she says, of where the father failed and was more concerned about himself. Having listened to his evidence, it was perfectly plain that what he told me was true. In fact, it seemed to me that he was genuinely anxious to assist his wife when she was unwell and genuinely anxious to get back to be with his son. He regretted, I thought genuinely, that she felt and feels the way that she did about those examples that she raised."

UK High Court Judge – Family Division, 2021.-Parental Alienation decision against mother in a fact-finding hearing.

44

Staying Strong

As I sit here writing this chapter, my journey is definitely not over. I must remain strong and hopeful. Too many women give up, die, kill themselves, or are pushed into repeat trauma while the family justice system watches, or in some cases, can be seen as participating in accelerating that harm.

I refuse to be one of those statistics.

You might ask why I have written this. Yes, I am very vulnerable putting this on paper given that I am *still* embroiled in the family justice system.

It feels to me like they have unfettered power with very little accountability. And it feels like they are going to do whatever they want, regardless of whatever consideration my children or I need.

Treatment of mothers has been noted as being borderline 'inhumane' in some cases, even being criticised for hugging her own children. And I have experienced that women and mothers can be judged more harshly. And given that this is *still* not over, that's why the only thing I can do going forward is to make sure I remain strong and calm, notwithstanding what may be done to me and my children.

"Some of the criticism of the Mother's conduct was not merely unfair, it bordered on the inhumane. The Mother was denied any contact with her children between March and July 20xx. When she was told in June that X was at the school fence very much wanting to see her mother she went and gave X a hug. She was criticised in cross examination for acting inappropriately by breaking 'the rules'. I consider that the Mother acted as any loving parent in her situation would have done. Somewhere in the history of this case we have lost our humanity."[34]

Warwickshire v Mother & Ors, 2023

45

Light at the End of the Tunnel

Has my journey ended? No. But my relationship with it has.

Domestic abuse is all about fear and control and I have reached a stage where I acknowledge that Prince Harming will continue to be disruptive and breach anything he is asked to do; and it seems to me that the system will continue to enable him.

I choose not to react whilst the abuse continues to be unacknowledged through the family justice system, as well.

I experienced being pushed from pillar to post, between social workers and family therapists, an experience that is well-documented and shared by many women on the same journey.

The system seems incapable of accommodating traumatised women. I am still being required to sit in a room with Prince Harming – the person who used to abuse; and 'detain' me in locked rooms. The immense distress that victims of abuse experience in facing their abusers is well-documented and accepted. My refusal to sit in a room with him is based on my truth that being in his presence triggers my anxiety and a visceral fear based on years of traumatic abuse.

The thought of being in a room with the person that used to systematically lock me in rooms year after year while ranting and screaming at me triggers anxiety and panic attacks.

All of this under the guise of 'family therapy'.

It feels like no one in the process seems to be assuming any responsibility for the potential harm they are exposing me to. The process seems to lack empathy and Practice Direction 12J or PD12J (the guidelines courts are recommended to consider in family cases alleging domestic abuse) seemingly overlooked.

'PD12J is reasonably comprehensive guidance, however, despite this and the mandatory nature of many of its provisions, the Family Court was still proving to be unsafe for adult and child victims and survivors, therefore undermining the Family Procedure Rules that apply when the most vulnerable legal subjects are implicated.

'The Harm Panel Report in June 2020 found that, due to deep seated and systemic failings, domestic abuse allegations and related risks to adult and child victims and survivors were not sufficiently taken into account by the Family Court when making contact arrangements for children, meaning that the courts were failing to adequately assess risks to children and protect them from harm.'

'Furthermore, the Harm Panel Report found that PD12J was not being consistently followed in practice. The report found that many judges and other professionals in the family justice system did not fully understand domestic abuse, especially coercive control (which, compared to physical abuse, often manifests as a recurring pattern of low severity/high harm incidents rather than as acute high harm singular incidents), or the impact it has on children. Consequently, adult and child victims and survivors were being failed repeatedly.'

The Family Court and domestic abuse: achieving cultural change.

The Domestic Abuse Commissioner's second report on the Family Court and domestic abuse. July 2023. Presented to Parliament pursuant to section 8(6) of the Domestic Abuse Act 2021

As my frustration with the process subsides, my ability to see through the games has increased. I have now learnt not to react to the process. My priority is to stay healthy, avoid stress and to look after the children. Everyone else can do their best to find financial opportunity at our expense. I am focusing on me, my children and addressing the sustained trauma I now have from ten years of abuse and ongoing legal cases. My body has been processing continued stress for seventeen years, so I need to now heal that trauma. I think two lumps is enough for one lifetime!

I now have a better understanding of the system my children and I are part of and I share what has helped me and is still helping me navigate this madness and bias of the family justice system . I hope whoever is reading this feels some comfort in knowing you are not alone. Try not to let the madness that will undoubtedly play around you make you fear or doubt your experience. Your truth is important- even if people find it uncomfortable or inconvenient.

Only you know the hell you have trudged through, so having information is key to helping you survive. Others will not fully understand what you have endured, and some may not even care, which is why it is important that you keep fighting for yourself.

My message to those reading this is:

The black hole or tunnel we find ourselves in may feel endless, but maybe the words in this book may be a torch of hope to guide you through it. I wish I had been told how hard the journey would be. I do not regret taking it, however, for I have learned how strong I have become. I have learnt how every girl and woman should know they have the right to make their own decisions in life – to be empowered – to be free. We should support girls in understanding the importance of that because it may save their life one day.

Perhaps we have buffered and protected girls to help them learn only how to navigate the patriarchy and live within the rules that others have set for women and girls, a survival approach. Maybe we should now teach girls that they have the right to make their own decisions, define their own boundaries, and change the world they live in. What would we want for our own daughters?

Sitting here in recovery from the removal of a tumour, having had no time to fully rest before addressing the family justice system, is not OK. Women are not meant to be abused. Women should be free in their mind, in their decisions, and in who they want to be... We have waited so long for others to do that for us and maybe now is the time for us to free ourselves.

"Strength doesn't come from what you can do. It comes from overcoming the things you once thought you couldn't."

Rikki Rogers.

46

Closing Message: I Hear You

"Within the various systems there is a lack of empathy and understanding of just what it takes for an abused woman to be heard, seen and understood. Too often this abuse screams in silence, yet it is so profoundly and deafeningly loud, like after a sound has been made in a large space or that of a confined place long after the initial abuse has occurred. It continues to echo and continues to reverberate throughout the life and world of the individual.

And thus she continues …the abuse becomes her…. all-consuming every thought and every action is a direct reaction or inaction to the abuse caused… It has rattled and shaken her to her very core… She did not lose herself, from herself she was stolen, slowly taken away from who she was, meant to be, dreamed once of being and becoming…

Like a thief steals and takes that which does not belong to him, so she was stolen; her self-esteem, her confidence broken, her very essence of her being a woman, her soul crushed…

She did not lose herself... her *self* was stolen."

J. Pinder- Counsellor & Psychotherapist.

Part 4

The Supplement

Introduction

As I mentioned in chapter 20 of the book, one of the impediments of leaving abuse is not knowing how. This supplement seeks to provide information that may link different parts of the cycle of abuse and provide insight into the family justice system that you may encounter, along with questions you may wish to raise that may assist you so that you can identify potential hurdles along with how best to overcome them- and regaining some control over decisions that impact you and your children.

Acknowledging Abuse

When I managed to escape my marriage, for some time, I still did not understand that I was a victim/survivor of domestic abuse.

It takes a while to recognise what you have endured, particularly when you have normalised things to get through each day and have learnt to detach from the emotion of what is happening; all whilst internalising the stress of living on constant eggshells. Through support, guidance and lots of research, I am eventually beginning to understand my journey.

Do you look abused enough to be heard?

Involved in various court and family proceedings across two countries, now in my seventh year, whilst I was a far stronger woman at the time of the UK proceedings, having endured various dirty tactics and tricks in the endless family proceedings, I clearly did not present to the UK courts as the expected stereotypical... *abused woman.* And I was punished for it. Perhaps we should turn up to court with blood and bruises to be heard?[35]

> "Some staff members raised cases where judges questioned the truth of disclosures if survivors didn't fulfil stereotypes about a 'typical' domestic violence survivor. For example, one judge said that the survivor 'didn't look like a victim' because she wore make-up to court."[36]

What the courts fail to understand is that many women don't even make it to court because they have been defeated, have died, killed themselves or have never been given the support to get there... But when they do, if they have managed to get their life together, they should not be punished for it just because they may not present as the stereotypical abused woman. Hopefully there will be a change in culture to bring more empathy and understanding of the cycle of abuse instead of blind judgement.

The Multi-Agency Disconnect?

Whilst many agencies exist with useful ideas, support, regulations, and codes, it seems there is still a gap in multi-agency coordination to prevent victims/survivors falling through the cracks.

Or, we read a continued reference to lack of training of participants in the family justice system, but no-one can learn or be taught empathy, so how do we train a new culture? Technology has made advances in every other field, perhaps it can be used for better training- perhaps Virtual Reality (VR) or Metaverse simulations where you may be able to feel and understand what domestic abuse feels like? Maybe that is what is missing?

Where laws, regulations and codes have been created against domestic abuse, it may need judges and courts to acknowledge domestic abuse e in order for other participants in the system to implement those laws required to safeguard the victim-survivor. If the abuse has already been minimised or dismissed at the outset by one court or process, how will those well-intentioned laws and regulations be applied to protect by another court or agency? Until there is better connection across the entire system, abuse will continue.

The Assessing Risk of Harm to Children and Parents in Private Law Children Cases or the 'Harm Report', June 2020, noted this practice of working in silos which:

> '...highlighted differences in approaches and culture between criminal justice, child protection (public law) and private law children proceedings, and lack of communication and coordination between family courts and other courts and agencies working with families, which led to contradictory decisions and confusion. Silo working can result in evidence of abuse accepted in one system, for example the criminal courts, not being acknowledged or effectively engaged with in the family court'.[37]

Understanding The Process

I was not prepared for what was to come, had no knowledge of the bias, and no understanding of how domestic abuse is minimised or disregarded by the family justice system participants – the process and options not explained. I was just another person in the process. Whilst it may be too late for me, I have gathered information that may be helpful to others.

Whilst much of what is set out in the law and supporting guidance may still not be followed as reported by various official sources, or whether allegations of domestic abuse continue to be undermined, minimised or dismissed as being in the victims mind or narrative only, it has helped me to understand the process much better. To know that your experiences are real, even if the truth may just be too inconvenient for some others.

After being controlled, undermined or crippled by fear, control and fear being key components of abuse, taking back some degree of control over your understanding of the process may help to take away some of the fear of it...

Who's Fighting Our Corner?

In a report published by Soroptimist International, it was noted that:

'...domestic abuse has been widespread in England and Wales, little acknowledged and, until 1976 when Jo Richardson MP introduced a Bill about it into Parliament, not regarded as a public matter. Her Bill allowed applications to the family courts for protective orders, in an attempt to make up for the criminal justice system's failure to tackle the harm done by perpetrators. It was almost 20 years until there was further legislation, but domestic abuse moved seriously nearer to the centre of the stage *only after the election of over 100 women MPs in the 1997 General Election*'.[38]

Victims/survivors should also consider reaching out to their local MP's, especially any female MP's who may be more understanding of the issues women are facing and may be more open to raising the problems you are facing to government-after all, it was *only when 100+ females were elected to government that the law started changing to protect women!*

Supplement Contents

This supplement provides some information that may help gain better understanding of the current state of the family justice system and various references and extracts that may be useful when navigating various stages of the cycle of abuse- this is not legal or financial advice, and may only be summary or extracts of wider documents, so you may wish to review the full information:

1. Domestic Abuse: What is it and How to Recognise it – UK Government.
2. 2. Domestic Abuse Act 2021 (UK) Useful to review the current Domestic Abuse law that may be referred to in legal matters:
3. Practice Direction 12J- Guidance that UK courts should consider in child arrangements in cases of alleged domestic abuse and harm.
4. Economic & Financial Abuse- Surviving Economic Abuse (SEA) / UK government Economic Abuse Toolkit.
5. Assessing Risk of Harm to Children and Parents in Private Law Children Cases 'Harm Report' (June 2020) – Report issued by the UK Ministry of Justice on problems and systemic weakness in the family justice system, including minimising domestic abuse.
6. Assessing Risk of Harm to Children and Parents in Private Law Children Cases 'Harm Report'- Implementation & Delivery Update (May 2023) – UK Ministry of Justice update

report confirming weaknesses in the family justice system and weaknesses in social workers and planned changes.

7. Social Work England- Principles that apply to social workers.

8. Preparing for court- authors checklist.

9. Child Proceedings- authors checklist.

10. Parental Alienation- UN report and others

11. UN Report of the Special Rapporteur on violence against women and girls, its causes and consequences, April 2023 – Custody, violence against women and violence against children – including concerns about parental alienation to silence domestic abuse allegations.

12. Survival Checklist- authors checklist.

I

Domestic Abuse: What Is It And How To Recognise It.

The table below summarises the categories of domestic abuse as listed by the UK Government.[39]

Emotional Abuse	Does your partner, or former partner, ever: • Belittle you, or put you down? • Blame you for the abuse or arguments? • Deny that abuse is happening, or play it down? • Isolate you from your family and friends? • Stop you going to college or work? • Make unreasonable demands for your attention? • Accuse you of flirting or having affairs? • Tell you what to wear, who to see, where to go, and what to think? • Control your money, or not give you enough to buy food or other essential things.
Threats & Intimidation	Does your partner, or former partner, ever: • Threaten to hurt or kill you? • Destroy things that belong to you? • Stand over you, invade your personal space? • Threaten to kill themselves or the children? • Read your emails, texts or letters? • Harass or follow you?
Physical Abuse	The person abusing you may hurt you in a number of ways. Does your partner, or former partner, ever: • Slap, hit or punch you? • Push or shove you? • Bite or kick you?

Physical Abuse *(continued)*	• Burn you? • Choke you or hold you down? • Throw things at you?
Sexual Abuse	Sexual abuse can happen to anyone, whether they're male or female. Does your partner, or former partner, ever: • Touch you in a way you don't want to be touched? • Make unwanted sexual demands? • Hurt you during sex? • Pressure you to have unsafe sex – for example, not using a condom? • Pressure you to have sex? • If your partner, or former partner, has sex with you when you don't want to, this is rape. • Have you ever felt afraid of your partner or former partner? • Have you ever changed your behaviour because you're afraid of what your partner, or former partner, might do?

2. Domestic Abuse Act 2021 (UK)[40]

Useful to review the current Domestic Abuse law.

Section 1: Definition of 'domestic abuse':

(1) This section defines "domestic abuse" for the purposes of this Act.

(2) Behaviour of a person ("A") towards another person ("B") is 'domestic abuse' if— (a) A and B are each aged sixteen or over and are 'personally connected' to each other, and (b) the behaviour is abusive.

(3) Behaviour is 'abusive' if it consists of any of the following—

(a) physical or sexual abuse.

(b) violent or threatening behaviour.

(c) controlling or coercive behaviour.

(d) economic abuse (see subsection (4)).

(e) psychological, emotional or other abuse; and

It does not matter whether the behaviour consists of a single incident or a course of conduct.

(4) 'Economic abuse' means any behaviour that has a substantial adverse effect on B's ability to —

(a) acquire, use or maintain money or other property, or

(b) obtain goods or services.

(5) For the purposes of this Act, A's behaviour may be behaviour "towards" B despite the fact that it consists of conduct directed at another person (for example, B's child).

Section 3: Children as Victims of Domestic Abuse

(1) This section applies where behaviour of a person ("A") towards another person ("B") is domestic abuse.

(2) Any reference in this Act to a victim of domestic abuse includes a reference to a child who –

(a) sees or hears, or experiences the effect of, the abuse, and
(b) is related to A or B.

(3) A child is related to a person for the purposes of subsection (2) if – (a) the person is a parent of, or has parental responsibility for, the child, or (b) the child and the person are relatives.

3. Practice Direction 12–J - Child Arrangements & Contact Orders: Domestic Abuse And Harm

Practice Direction 12J[41] is part of the Family Procedure Rules providing guidance for the courts to consider. These are rules that set out the way the court should deal with or consider family cases in relation to child arrangements where there are allegations of domestic abuse and harm.

For the purpose of this Practice Direction 'the 2021 Act' means the Domestic Abuse Act 2021. Sections 3 and 4 include the following guidance and useful definitions).

Coercive behaviour	Coercive behaviour means an act or a pattern of acts of assault, threats, humiliation and intimidation or other abuse that is used to harm, punish, or frighten the victim.
Controlling behaviour	Controlling behaviour means an act or pattern of acts designed to make a person subordinate and/or dependent by isolating them from sources of support, exploiting their resources and capacities for personal gain, depriving them of the means needed for independence, resistance and escape and regulating their everyday behaviour.
Harm	Harm means ill-treatment or the impairment of health or development including, for example, impairment suffered from seeing or hearing the ill-treatment of another, by domestic abuse or otherwise.
Ill Treatment	Ill-treatment includes sexual abuse and forms of ill-treatment which are not physical.

Victim	Victim of domestic abuse' includes, but is not limited to, a child who is a victim of domestic abuse by virtue of section 3 of the 2021 Act.
Domestic Abuse and children	Domestic abuse is harmful to children, and/or puts children at risk of harm, including where they are victims of domestic abuse for example by witnessing one of their parents being violent or abusive to the other parent, or living in a home in which domestic abuse is perpetrated (even if the child is too young to be conscious of the behaviour). Children may suffer direct physical, psychological and/or emotional harm from living with and being victims of domestic abuse and may also suffer harm indirectly where the domestic abuse impairs the parenting capacity of either or both of their parents.

4. Economic & Financial Abuse

Economic And Financial Abuse Domestic Abuse can also and quite often involves economic and financial abuse. It takes many forms, the objective may include various outcomes, dependency, control, intimidation, fear and/or making it harder for women to leave the abuse and more. The information below is provided from the UK Government sources and Surviving Economic Abuse as economic abuse is now part of the Domestic Abuse Act 2021. Financial Abuse is also included as a form of abuse in Section 42 (3) of the Care Act (2014).

Understand:

(4) "Economic abuse"[42] means any behaviour that has a substantial adverse effect on B's ability to —

(a) acquire, use or maintain money or other property, or

(b) obtain goods or services.

(5) For the purposes of this Act, A's behaviour may be behaviour 'towards B despite the fact that it consists of conduct directed at another person (for example, B's child).

As per the UK government economic abuse toolkit,[43] economic abuse generally falls under three categories:

Restriction	The abuser insists on seeing receipts or running through bank statements line-by-line, making the victim-survivor ask to use utilities, the car, a mobile phone etc.
Exploitation	The abuser pawning/selling the victim-survivor's belongings, stealing their savings, making them work but taking their wages, insisting all liabilities are in the victim-survivor's name, refusing to contribute to household costs, and building up debts in the victim-survivor's name.
Sabotage	The abuser destroying belongings, preventing the victim-survivor from being in education or employment, limiting their working hours which can cause them to lose their job, refusing to let them claim benefits and refusing to let them access a bank account.

Economic abuse in effect – possible example

An abuser may use the victim-survivor's credit cards or other financial products to pay for their own lifestyle. Due to fear of consequences, the victim-survivor can do nothing. The abuser will run up large bills, which the victim-survivor has to cover by having to work harder to earn more money or face going into debt. As a result they may become more tired and more controllable.

An abuser may not work but instead live off a victim-survivor, giving the impression of working but actually contributing little. For example, this may take place through a joint business venture. Here an abuser often creates a situation where the victim-survivor is working constantly to pay off debts and bills, while earning money to stay alive, which can lead to dependence and/or exhaustion.

Surviving Economic Abuse (SEA)

Surviving Economic Abuse (SEA) sets out further information on economic and financial abuse.

Economic Abuse is now becoming a recognised issue and concern with many global banks presenting strong marketing campaigns to raise awareness of the issue- including the global bank that thwarted my access to my records and tipping off my ex-husband, but nonetheless, economic abuse happens in many forms, such as restriction, sabotage, controlling the economic position of women- examples include:

- Controlling the wealth a woman may have.
- Stopping women from accessing funds or working.
- Stopping a woman becoming financially independent.
- Preventing women making financial decisions.
- Obstructing child maintenance payments.
- Prolonging court processes to diminish a woman's funds.
- Preventing women from having independent bank accounts and bank facilities.
- Coerced debt (women being pushed into taking debt facilities and the funds being used by the abuser).
- Refusal to pay mortgage or rental payments.
- Refusal to make payments in joint account situations resulting in debt breaches, CCJ's being put in the name of women making it difficult to obtain bank services in the future.

Economic & Financial Abuse
Child Maintenance as a tool for coercive control

> "Withholding child maintenance or making payments unreliably is a common form of economic abuse that takes place after a relationship has ended. It is a tool for coercive control that can have a significant effect on victim-survivors. It can affect their ability to provide for their children and build economic safety after leaving an abuser."[45,46]

Withholding, delaying, or reducing working hours to manipulate child maintenance is another key tool to continue to exert control. The law, described below, is being updated to remove direct engagement with the abuser when collecting child maintenance and further laws are being discussed to strengthen the enforcement against abusers for using child maintenance to economically abuse victims-survivors.

Child Support Collection (Domestic Abuse) Act.
Passed 29th June 2023

The new child support collection law will allow the Child Maintenance Service (CMS)[46] to use its powers to collect and make payments on behalf of parents where one of them requests for this on the grounds of domestic abuse.

Victim-survivors will now be able to request Collect and Pay, without having to get agreement from the abuser or prove that the abuser is unlikely to pay child maintenance.

These changes are very recent so will still require appropriate understanding and change in culture and willingness to show empathy by those involved in the family justice system to support the prompt application of the law, for example, how will domestic abuse be recognised to enable a women to seek the protection in this new law if reports still show dismissal of allegations of abuse by the courts? What evidence of abuse will be required for women to be able to seek support to use these protections in this law?

Seen Yet Sidelined[47]

Surviving Economic Abuse (SEA) noted that the issue of EconomicAbuse is still challenging to prosecute particularly within the coercive and controlling behaviour offence even though most police forces are now putting more cases forward. Warning signs of economic abuse and other forms of non-physical abuse still need to be recognised more widely to support early recognition and intervention so that cases are, in turn, prosecuted earlier and do not escalate to the levels described within the news reports analysed.

SEA recommends that Police guidance on the Controlling or Coercive Behaviour Offence should ensure that responding officers are aware of the many different forms that economic abuse takes. Police training needs to equip officers to be able to establish whether there are patterns of controlling or coercive behaviours underlying the incident that led to a police callout as well the ability to proactively recognise and identify the signs of coercive control, including economic control when a victim-survivor is making a statement and may be alluding to these behaviours within their description of the circumstances

Focussing on physical violence only without considering non-physical abuse or considering the historical abuse may result in the abuse continuing.

We all need to raise awareness.

5. Assessing Risk of Harm to Children and Parents in Private Law Children Cases 'Harm Report' (June 2020) – UK Ministry of Justice[48]

In June 2020, the UK Ministry of Justice published a final report of its expert panel on assessing risk of harm to children and parents in private family law children cases.

Following a public call for evidence, the report noted, among other items, that '...the family courts do not effectively protect many child and adult victims of domestic abuse from further harm'.

The evidence received by the panel, together with the literature review, identified four overarching barriers to the family court's ability to respond consistently and effectively to domestic abuse and other serious offences:

1. The court's pro-contact culture
2. The adversarial system
3. Resource limitations affecting all aspects of private law proceedings
4. The way the family court works in silo, lacking coordination with other courts and organisations dealing with domestic abuse.

The pro-contact culture of the courts and professionals involved in child arrangement cases; submissions highlighted a resulting lack of understanding of the different forms that domestic abuse takes, and of the ongoing impacts of abuse on children and victim parents, the systematic minimisation or disbelief of abuse, and the acceptance of counter-allegations without robust scrutiny.

Some of the key highlights of the report are set out below:

Evidencing Abuse	Victims reported difficulties evidencing abuse, particularly where there was a focus on single incidents or recent physical abuse, and where they encountered stereotypical views of how an 'ideal victim' should behave.
Children's Voices	Pro-contact culture. Submissions identified a process of 'selective listening', whereby children who wish to have contact with their non-resident parent are heard but those who do not wish to have contact are not heard or pressured to change their views. Orders were reported as often prioritising a child spending time with a potentially abusive parent regardless of their particular circumstances.
Silo Working	Submissions highlighted that courts often failed to engage effectively with organisations that had established strong relationships with a child and may have a more in-depth knowledge of their individual circumstances. Evidence suggested that there are significant negative impacts to children being unheard during proceedings. Children can be left feeling let down or suspicious of authorities, and trust in the court system can be eroded due to a child's negative experiences.
Dependence on the court is discouraged - Orders made	Submissions and previous file studies indicate that consent orders are made on a regular basis; victims of abuse may feel pressured to agree to such orders even when they do not consider them to be safe. Review hearings, which might provide a check on the workability and safety of orders, are discouraged and rarely take place.

Harm Arising from Family Court Orders	Respondents felt that orders made by the court had enabled the continued control and/or abuse of children and adult victims of domestic abuse by alleged abusers.. Submissions detailed the long-term impacts of this abuse manifesting in physical, emotional, psychological, financial and educational harm and harm to children's current and future relationships. Respondents felt that the level of abuse they and their children experienced worsened following proceedings in the family court.
Impact on other agencies as a result of family court orders	Efforts to report continuing abuse were treated dismissively by criminal justice and child welfare agencies because of the family court orders. Respondents highlighted the negative impacts felt by children who were compelled to have contact with abusive parents, and the burden placed on mothers and children to comply with contact orders compared to minimal expectations on perpetrators of abuse to change their behaviour.
Social Workers	Reports issued by the UK Ministry of Justice, concluded that there was a significant weakness in the knowledge and skills of social workers who are undertaking risk assessments and other related direct work with children and their families where domestic abuse is alleged, suspected or known. The panel has recommended that social workers undertaking assessments for private law children's proceedings in Wales are trained in domestic abuse to Group 3 Violence Against Women, Domestic Abuse and Sexual Violence National Training Framework standard. An update on the status of this recommendation is pending.

6. Assessing Risk of Harm to Children and Parents in Private Law Children Cases -Implementation Plan: delivery update – UK Ministry of Justice, May 2023[49]

In 2023, a follow up report was issued to consider the implementation plan to reform the weaknesses identified in the original 'Harm Report' and it was again restated that:

> "Despite finding some good practice and well-intentioned staff, the Panel exposed deep-seated systemic failings which, in the worst cases, put victims of domestic abuse and their children at risk. The Panel found that too often, adversarial court proceedings retraumatised victims. Allegations of domestic abuse were too readily disbelieved or dismissed, alongside poor risk assessments and siloed working. The report also identified a view amongst many respondents that courts often placed an undue emphasis on ensuring children had contact with both parents."

Victim/Survivor and Perpetrator Experience[50]

The 'Harm Report' presented information on the perspective victim/survivors and perpetrators of Domestic Abuse in the family justice system.

The negative view of domestic abuse held by the family justice system, presents a potentially positive outcome for the perpetrator whilst a negative for the victim/survivor, some of these views being set before the process has even begun:

Domestic Abuse Perpetrators' Experience

(Likely to produce favourable outcomes for perpetrators.)

Courts do not like to hear about domestic abuse.	The panel received a number of submissions from individual lawyers about their experiences in child contact cases. Some of these submissions indicated that lawyers have advised their clients not to raise domestic abuse because it would 'anger' the courts or be 'counter-productive'.
Protecting abusers with their behaviour dismissed, condoned or justified through the courts/ enabling further abuse.	One respondent observed one of the magistrates appearing to collude with the perpetrator by 'sniggering' with him. Overall, she stated that the magistrates: 'validated and normalised my ex-husband's abusive behaviour…[overlooking]…glaring contradictions in his evidence'. As a result she felt that the court 'effectively made the abuser feel supported by the court and protected from further consequences'
Protecting abusers who present as calm	It is perhaps easy to see how the courts and other professionals might find an abuser to be more believable when they appear calm, well presented and 'reasonable'.
Protecting abusers that become abusive during court process	The submissions included some examples of abusers becoming verbally and physically aggressive in the court building and even in the courtroom itself. In some instances judges and court staff were said to have 'made excuses' for such behaviour. The panel was told of abusive behaviour being regarded as 'justified' as an understandable result of the frustration at lack of contact and the mother's perceived hostility to contact in some cases

Lack of understanding of domestic abuse/ focus on recent incidents only	A common theme emerging from the mothers' submissions was that all the agencies, particularly Cafcass/Cymru and the courts, were only concerned with incidents of domestic abuse that had occurred in recent months or weeks. 'Historical' allegations were treated as less relevant and victims were sometimes discouraged or prevented from talking about the cumulative effect of abuse going back over a number of years. Even if domestic abuse does cease, its psychological effects are likely to be felt for even longer.
Courts do not like to hear about domestic abuse.	The panel received a number of submissions from individual lawyers about their experiences in child contact cases. Some of these submissions indicated that lawyers have advised their clients not to raise domestic abuse because it would 'anger' the courts or be 'counter-productive'.
Dismissing victim/ survivors- Legal professionals pushing victim/ survivors into settlements to avoid court.	The evidence suggests that some lawyers do encourage their clients towards settlement in such a way that minimises or dismisses domestic abuse.
Dismissing domestic abuse in cases where there was a lack of evidence of physical abuse	A case was heard by the magistrates, the mother said she felt that the court were not interested in the abuse and 'attempted to bat away the issue of abuse because I did not have broken bones or physical bruises to show them.' In her view the court were 'shockingly and dangerously dismissive of serious concerns of domestic abuse'.

Domestic Abuse Victim/Survivors' Experience

(Likely to minimise or undermine the victim/survivor's experience.)

Discriminating against women and victim/ survivors who do not appear calm.	Some of the submissions from mothers told of how they felt seriously disadvantaged by appearing emotional and disordered.
Discriminating against women and victim/ survivors who do appear calm	The panel received a number of submissions from individual lawyers about their experiences in child contact cases. Submissions indicated that lawyers have advised their clients not to raise domestic abuse because it would 'anger' the courts or be 'counter-productive'.
Dismissing victim/ survivors- Legal professionals pushing victim/ survivors into settlements to avoid court.	Professional submissions also revealed the no-win situation abused women may face. Submissions from Welsh Women's Aid and others stated that in cases where the mother was calm, clear and articulate in court they were also disbelieved by judges.
Children not heard	Voices of children go unheard in the court process or are muted in various ways. The panel found that a significant number of children who have experienced domestic abuse are not consulted on their views and experiences during the court process. Many submissions observed that consultations are brief, and that children are only 'heard' when they express a wish to have contact. The panel found that children are rarely consulted on how arrangements are working for them once an order has been made.
Dismissing domestic abuse by reframing domestic abuse as a 'high conflict' case	The panel was told that, on occasions, the mother's own lawyers advised them not to raise allegations for these reasons. There was evidence of domestic abuse being relabelled as 'high conflict' relationships.

Dismissing victim/ survivors of domestic abuse and incident reporting to police- women disbelieved for failing to report domestic abuse to the police or ignored when incidents were reported to the police	Mothers' submissions to the panel stated that they were questioned about why they had not reported allegations to the police and were either told, or got the strong impression, that they were not believed because they had not made a call to the police. However, even in cases where there was evidence from the police, this was not always considered to be relevant. The panel was told by several mothers that they had reported incidents to the police but when they tried to introduce this as evidence in the family courts it was dismissed or disregarded.
Women that do not look like victims of domestic abuse disbelieved	Some staff members raised cases where judges questioned the truth of disclosures if survivors didn't fulfil stereotypes about a 'typical' domestic violence survivor. For example, one judge said that the survivor 'didn't look like a victim' because she wore make-up to court... Staff said that in their experience when survivors had difficulty communicating the abuse, sometimes breaking down or crying, this was looked upon negatively by the court. Some staff members perceived some judges' attitudes towards survivors as 'this is an emotionally temperamental woman' rather than 'this is an abused and traumatised woman', dismissing either the allegations, or their relevance'. Refuge

7. Social Work England- Professional Standards Applicable To Social Workers[51]

Where children are involved, social workers will be engaged in the process, their role should be to act in the welfare of the children and family, wherever possible. However, there are many instances where social workers interaction may raise questions of professional boundaries and their 'fitness to practise'.

My own child was also sent to contact sick, my concerns about my child being sick ignored, I was also contacted a few days after my own surgery following a legal request not to continue silo conversations with the father – (all ignored) and so on. Social workers carry significant power in the family process, sometimes it may feel like there is little or no accountability that accompanies that power.

If you have concerns about the social worker, the below table may assist in ensuring your concerns relate to a specific standard that the social worker must comply with- raising general concerns about bias or conflict of interest may not be considered.

The below may be an example to assist with records of interactions with social workers:

Name of Social Worker	Registration Number

This submission is made to raise concerns about fitness to practise for alleged breach of professional boundaries as explained below:

Date of Incident (DD/MM/YYYY)	Evidence	Related Professional Standard
X October 2021 X April 2022 X May 2023 X May 2023 X June 2023	Legal notes, statement of XX, contact note dated XX noting that: XX has made poor notes, forgotten the details and will no longer use discretion to avoid facts being left out of notes, unable to confirm if mother's location was inadvertently disclosed as noted in submissions made to court.	2.2 2.4 2.6 3.4 3.11
X September 2021	Meeting with Child Y and after pushing him to communicate with father and that Child Y had no choice, XX ceased with the questioning when Child Y began to cry. XX then left Child Y- informed the mother that the child was crying and asked for a lift to the train station- leaving Child Y upset and distressed. *(Continues)*	

X September 2021 *(Continued)*	Evidence: XX own notes confirming incident. Evidence: email of concern from school of Child Y of bias and questioning approach of XX which the school found uncomfortable/ unprofessional.

Social Work England

Summary of applicable professional standards:[52]

Standard	Detail
1. Promote the rights, strengths and wellbeing of people, families and communities	As a social worker, I will: 1.1 Value each person as an individual, recognising their strengths and abilities. 1.2 Respect and promote the human rights, views, wishes and feelings of the people I work with, balancing rights and risks and enabling access to advice, advocacy, support and services. 1.3 Work in partnership with people to promote their well-being and achieve best outcomes, recognising them as experts in their own lives. 1.4 Value the importance of family and community systems and work in partnership with people to identify and harness the assets of those systems. 1.5 Recognise differences across diverse communities and challenge the impact of disadvantage and discrimination on people and their families and communities. 1.6 Promote social justice, helping to confront and resolve issues of inequality and inclusion. 1.7 Recognise and use responsibly, the power and authority I have when working with people, ensuring that my interventions are always necessary, the least intrusive, proportionate, and in people's best interests.

Standard	Detail
2. Establish and maintain the trust and confidence of people	As a social worker, I will: 2.1 Be open, honest, reliable and fair. 2.2 Respect and maintain people's dignity and privacy. 2.3 Maintain professional relationships with people and ensure that they understand the role of a social worker in their lives. 2.4 Practise in ways that demonstrate empathy, perseverance, authority, professional confidence and capability, working with people to enable full participation in discussions and decision making. 2.5 Actively listen to understand people, using a range of appropriate communication methods to build relationships. 2.6 Treat information about people with sensitivity and handle confidential information in line with the law. 2.7 Consider where conflicts of interest may arise, declare conflicts as early as possible and agree a course of action.
3. Be accountable for the quality of my practice and the decisions I make	As a social worker, I will: 3.1 Work within legal and ethical frameworks, using my professional authority and judgement appropriately. 3.2 Use information from a range of appropriate sources, including supervision, to inform assessments, to analyse risk, and to make a professional decision.

Standard	Detail
3. Be accountable *(Continued)*	3.3 Apply my knowledge and skills to address the social care needs of individuals and their families commonly arising from physical and mental ill health, disability, substance misuse, abuse or neglect, to enhance quality of life and wellbeing. 3.4 Recognise the risk indicators of different forms of abuse and neglect and their impact on people, their families and their support networks. 3.5 Hold different explanations in mind and use evidence to inform my decisions. 3.6 Draw on the knowledge and skills of workers from my own and other professions and work in collaboration, particularly in integrated teams, holding onto and promoting my social work identity. 3.7 Recognise where there may be bias in decision making and address issues that arise from ethical dilemmas, conflicting information, or differing professional decisions. 3.8 Clarify where the accountability lies for delegated work and fulfil that responsibility when it lies with me. 3.9 Make sure that relevant colleagues and agencies are informed about identified risks and the outcomes and implications of assessments and decisions I make. 3.10 Establish and maintain skills in information and communication technology and adapt my practice to new ways of working, as appropriate.

Standard	Detail
3. Be accountable *(Continued)*	3.11 Maintain clear, accurate, legible and up to date records, documenting how I arrive at my decisions. 3.12 Use my assessment skills to respond quickly to dangerous situations and take any necessary protective action. 3.13 Provide, or support people to access advice and services tailored to meet their needs, based on evidence, negotiating and challenging other professionals and organisations, as required. 3.14 Assess the influence of cultural and social factors over people and the effect of loss, change and uncertainty in the development of resilience. 3.15 Recognise and respond to behaviour that may indicate resistance to change, ambivalent or selective cooperation with services, and recognise when there is a need for immediate action.
4. Maintain my continuing professional development	As a social worker, I will: 4.1 Incorporate feedback from a range of sources, including from people with lived experience of my social work practice. 4.2 Use supervision and feedback to critically reflect on, and identify my learning needs, including how I use research and evidence to inform my practice. 4.3 Keep my practice up to date and record how I use research, theories and frameworks to inform my practice and my professional judgement.

Standard	Detail
4. Maintain my continuing professional development *(Continued)*	4.4 Demonstrate good subject knowledge on key aspects of social work practice and develop knowledge of current issues in society and social policies impacting on social work. 4.5 Contribute to an open and creative learning culture in the workplace to discuss, reflect on and share best practice. 4.6 Reflect on my learning activities and evidence what impact continuing professional development has on the quality of my practice. 4.7 Record my learning and reflection on a regular basis and in accordance with Social Work England's guidance on continuing professional development. 4.8 Reflect on my own values and challenge the impact they have on my practice.
5. Act safely, respectfully and with professional integrity	As a social worker, I will not: 5.1 Abuse, neglect, discriminate, exploit or harm anyone, or condone this by others. 5.2 Behave in a way that would bring into question my suitability to work as a social worker while at work, or outside of work. 5.3 Falsify records or condone this by others. 5.4 Ask for, or accept any money, gifts or hospitality which may affect or appear to affect my professional judgement. 5.5 Treat someone differently because they've raised a complaint.

Standard	Detail
5. Act safely... *(Continued)*	5.6 Use technology, social media or other forms of electronic communication unlawfully, unethically, or in a way that brings the profession into disrepute.
6. Promote ethical practice and report concerns	As a social worker, I will: 6.1 Report allegations of harm and challenge and report exploitation and any dangerous, abusive or discriminatory behaviour or practice. 6.2 Reflect on my working environment and where necessary challenge practices, systems and processes to uphold Social Work England's professional standards. 6.3 Inform people of the right to complain and provide them with the support to do it, and record and act on concerns raised to me. 6.4 Take appropriate action when a professional's practice may be impaired. 6.5 Raise concerns about organisational wrongdoing and cultures of inappropriate and unsafe practice. 6.6 Declare to the appropriate authority and Social Work England anything that might affect my ability to do my job competently or may affect my fitness to practise, or if I am subject to criminal proceedings or a regulatory finding is made against me, anywhere in the world. 6.7 Cooperate with any investigations by my employer, Social Work England, or another agency, into my fitness to practise or the fitness to practise of others.

8. Preparing for Court

Preparing for Court Whilst this process can be very daunting, it is important to list key events factually and succinctly with dates and any evidence that you can reference.

As hard as it may be, there is very little empathy in the system, so your facts will be critical in the process, don't be surprised if you are also heavily criticised for having strong facts and evidence, like I was, but it is important to have your evidence to back up everything you put forward, the standard is much higher for women, especially when alleging domestic abuse. Even if victims/survivors may be disregarded or their evidence minimised, it is important to have the information prepared, such as below:

An Incident Table is needed once you have clearly decided that you are the recipient of repeated domestic abuse (physical and/or non physical); contemplating an exit from that relationship; most likely to require legal services; and it is highly probable that you will need to make court appearances i.e., child custody, child protection etc.

I would emphasise that you would need to consider how you archive and retrieve these incidents especially if you are being monitored closely.

I would emphasise that if you seek assistance i.e., medical, that you keep accurate records of visits to doctors, for example.

Incident Table Example

Date of Incident Start-End Date	Title of the incident	Description of the incident	Evidence	Notes/ Reminders
Started May 2021 (Approx 2pm) Ended May 2021 (Approx 3.30pm)	Locked in room and physically hit	I was led into a room which he locked behind me and he began verbally abusing me and cornering me until I fell. I could not breathe and felt dizzy and then he kicked me.	1. SMS dated XX May 2021 2. Doctor's note confirming bruising	
Started June 2021 (Approx 8.345pm) Ended June 2021 (Approx 9pm)	Locked in house and keys removed	I was screamed at and pushed when I tried to get ready to go to work. He pushed me until I fell and then locked me in, took my phone and took the key. I was unable to leave the house and unable to go to work or call anyone.	3. Email with HR stating that I was on sick leave and could not come to work.	Prepare to be challenged as you will have no direct proof in this example.

9. Child Proceedings

If there are children involved, remain calm. I know this is hard as there will be many 'specialists' that may become involved and make critical decisions about you and your children.

Preparation and Research	Review the UK Ministry of Justice Harm Report (June 2020 and the Delivery Update (May 2023).[53] This may be uncomfortable to read, but it is useful to understand what you may encounter.
Prepare your Incident Table (See Section 8)	Prepare your own Incident Table (the example above may help)- this can then be shared with any lawyers to feed into any legal document that may be prepared for submission to court and may help you keep your position clear, summarised and with the points clear if representing yourself without a solicitor. Taking 'control' over your own legal case may be helpful as only you will fully understand what happened to you and this information may make it better for your lawyers to prepare your case and keep costs down. List incidents by date, when they started, when they ended and a clear description of the incident and provide any supporting evidence.
Make your own contact notes:	Before any contact co-ordinated through the social worker, I would prepare my own notes. That's right, I would prepare contact notes BEFORE the contact (details of eating venues left blank) I would then email these to myself because what I found was that the social worker was predictable in her note taking. *(Continues)*

Make your own contact notes *(Continued)*	I kept each contact note I prepared and emailed them to myself and my lawyer so there would be a clear date on it. This helped evidence the bias and deflection of any responsibility and assisted me to prove inaccuracies and errors in the social workers account of events. It also helped me not to feel so unheard by the social worker. The first couple of contact notes will usually provide a style that the social worker will adopt and also the social workers perspective of you. The social worker was critical of how close the children were with me and specifically noted, in the negative, how many times my son hugged and repeatedly turned and waved at me when he was taken to each contact - so I had to refrain from doing so at future contact arrangements to avoid undue criticism. This then creates an unnatural environment with the social worker, so have your own records.
Carefully check the social worker's notes after each contact:	Review the notes and highlight key points. This was very helpful as I tracked and recorded all the inconsistencies across the notes over the course of 12 months to avoid being accused of things that I did not say or do. It was a valuable exercise as it showed – in writing – the social worker's own inconsistencies and errors that I had been blamed for. Please also refer to the Social Work England Professional Standards (set out further in this book)- this may help if you feel concerned about the social worker in terms of their fitness to practise.[54]
Keep medical records of your children	On certain occasions my child was sent to contact sick- even though I raised this with the social worker before the contact, I was ignored. My child was subsequently diagnosed with a chest infection. *(Continues)*

Keep medical records of your children *(Continued)*	Whilst I felt helpless as a mother, it was very important to keep these communications even though both my child and I were ignored. The social worker defended the father (even though she herself was not part of that contact visit but her replacement), and until date the father still has not addressed our concerns about sickness and welfare of the child, even though the social worker, has independently communicated on behalf of the father with a message about the children's health which is inconsistent with the legal communications on the same matter from the father's legal representatives relating to a contact that she was not attending herself. That all needs to be noted carefully and referred to in and formal proceedings if needed.
Parental Alienation	Research *parental alienation* when children are involved as it is widely known that this will be used to diminish any claim of domestic abuse. It is the claim that one parent has turned the child against the other parent, resulting in resistance to contact. Even if there has been abuse, it will be minimised or disregarded to deflect from the abusers behaviour and is often used as a tactic to retain control through child contact arrangements, with potential threat of removing the child from the alienating parent (typically mothers being accused). This has been reported by the World Health Organisation (WHO), UN and other agencies as referenced in this document. There is also confusion around what a 'specialist' in this field noting that some practitioners refer to themselves as 'psychologist' which is a term that can be used by anyone, even if not fully qualified. (Refer Re C – Parental Alienation)[55,56]

10. Parental Alienation

Parental alienation is a very controversial concept used across the family justice system, globally. It has also been increasingly used to counter allegations of domestic abuse, to silence mothers.

It is a very lucrative business for those involved and subject to criticism by governments and more recently the UN. In cases where parental alienation is found, mothers can lose their custody and based on parental alienation 'specialists' being restricted from having any contact with their own children as part of forced reunification plans, where a complete 'cut-off' from the parent accused of parental alienation, which is mainly mothers, can be ordered.

Parental alienation is widely used to defend against allegations of domestic abuse, effectively 'gagging' mothers for fear of losing their own children.

In this section, the reference to UN means the 'UN Report Custody, violence against women and violence against children Report of the Special Rapporteur on violence against women and girls, its causes and consequences, April 2023'[57]

Parental Alienation – Possible Outcomes

1. Loss of custody- referred to as Transfer of Residence to 'alienated' parent.
2. Forced reunification with 'alienated' parent and complete 'cut-off' from 'alienating' parent (typically against the mother)
3. Limited contact with children that have been transferred to the 'alienated' parent.

As a result of the above, which are only some of the available outcomes, many mothers are advised or frightened to raise allegations of domestic abuse for fear of losing custody of their children.

Parental alienation has now become an industry for professionals and go to defence against domestic abuse allegations.[58,59,60]

Definitions of Parental Alienation

a. UN Reference,

Definition and use of the pseudo-concept of 'parental alienation'[2]

'... there is no commonly accepted clinical or scientific definition of 'parental alienation'. Broadly speaking, parental alienation is understood to refer to deliberate or unintentional acts that cause unwarranted rejection by the child towards one of the parents, usually the father'.

b. UK Cafcass defines Parental Alienation as:

We[62] define parental alienation as the unjustified resistance or hostility from a child towards one parent as a result of psychological manipulation by the other parent.

Origins of Parental Alienation

The UN Report further noted that:

> '... The pseudo-concept of parental alienation was coined by Richard Gardner, a psychologist, who claimed that children alleging sexual abuse during high conflict divorces suffer from 'parental alienation syndrome' caused by mothers who have led their children to believe that they have been abused by their fathers and to raise allegations of abuse against them. He recommended draconian remedies to address the syndrome, including a complete cut-off from the mother in order to 'deprogram' the child.

It was argued that the more that children rejected the relationship with their fathers, the more evidence of the alienating syndrome was observed. Gardner's theory has been criticized for its lack of empirical basis, for its problematic assertions about sexual abuse and for recasting abuse claims as false tools for alienation, which, in some cases, have dissuaded evaluators and courts from assessing whether abuse has actually occurred.

The UN report went further and noted the bias and misuse of Parental Alienation (PA):

> Findings from those reviewed cases also showed mothers had little to no success when claiming PA, despite evidence that the fathers were abusive and controlling, suggesting a one-sided dimension to PA.

The research identified a pattern of abusive parents, usually the father, accusing the parent with custody of alienating the children against them. In some instances, this became grounds for transfers of residence of the child.The research also raises questions about the purpose and use of PA in private law proceedings in the family courts.

Concern around specialists[63,64]

There is current some confusion about what a *psychologist* is, for example. According to the healthcare bodies, the term 'psychologist' is not protected and is being used by people that are not members of the relevant professional bodies. Caution has been raised to ensure that 'experts' are thoroughly vetted before permitted to give evidence, otherwise an unqualified professional can issue an influential report resulting in the loss of custody (as in Re C).

'Certain categories of psychologist, for example 'clinical psychologist,', have a 'protected title', which may only be used by those who are validly registered under the regulations. The generic label 'psychologist' is not protected and may be used by any individual, whether registered or not. A report by an unregistered person calling themselves a psychologist may be called a 'psychological report. ... it is ultimately a matter for the Government to determine which roles should be subject to statutory regulation'.

Re C- Parental Alienation

'... it is ultimately a matter for the Government to determine which roles should be subject to statutory regulation.'

The Domestic Abuse Commissioner's second report on the Family Court and domestic abuse also noted the following:

'Roundtable participants were particularly concerned about the use of experts (sometimes with recognised qualifications in psychology and psychotherapy and sometimes without) to draft reports for the court alleging that a child has been subjected to so-called 'parental' alienation, with these reports then being relied on by the judge. Some of these reports are extremely costly to obtain and mean that a parent who has more money, is able to obtain reports which may persuade the Family Court to make an order which is not in the best interests of the child.

Several pieces of correspondence to the Commissioner also raised concerns about these kinds of experts. In these cases, many roundtable participants impressed how the allegation of so-called 'parental' alienation appeared to supersede any presence of domestic abuse. The use of unregulated experts to this effect, is chilling, and their increasing presence has caused both fear and a lack of faith in the Family Court to address domestic abuse.'

The commissioner further made the following recommendation in her report which was addressed to Parliament:

'RECOMMENDATION 10

The Commissioner recommends the Ministry of Justice consult with her Office, the specialist domestic abuse sector, the relevant regulatory bodies, NHS England, NHS Wales, the specialist children's sector to develop a stricter definition of psychologist. The Ministry of Justice should identify an appropriate legislative opportunity to implement this definition.'

Role of Social Workers

Social workers play a key, and powerful, role in the family justice process. They are looked upon to be fair and just in the welfare of all those involved in the process, especially children.

However, there has been criticism and first-hand experiences of many mothers that social workers can show bias and lack empathy for both mothers and children. As reported below:

Social Workers

The Panel's report concluded that was a significant weakness in the knowledge and skills of social workers who are undertaking risk assessments and other related direct work with children and their families where domestic abuse is alleged, suspected or known'.

Assessing Risk of Harm to Children and Parents in Private Law Children Cases - Implementation Plan: delivery update - UK Ministry of Justice, May 2023[65]

Role Of The Evaluator In Family Courts[66]

'Parental alienation and related pseudo-concepts are embedded in the legal system, including amongst evaluators tasked with reporting to the family courts on the best interest of the child (psychiatrists, psychoanalysts, psychologists and social workers). Parental alienation has been endorsed through formal training and promulgated by professional networks and, more recently, academic journals.

'Parental alienation and related pseudo-concepts are embedded in the legal system, including amongst evaluators tasked with reporting to the family courts on the best interest of the child (psychiatrists, psychoanalysts, psychologists and social workers). Parental alienation has been endorsed through formal training and promulgated by professional networks and, more recently, academic journals.

The application of parental alienation has also been exacerbated by the lack of formal training for justice system professionals and the relationship between allegations of parental alienation and the dynamics of domestic violence. When faced with a dispute between parents, family courts often look to independent advice from child experts to decide on an appropriate outcome. While the ultimate decision is made by the presiding judge, the recommendation of the evaluator is powerful and one that, in practice, most judges follow. According to submissions received….. most allegations of parental alienation arise from reports of social workers...'

UN Report Custody, violence against women and violence against children Report of the Special Rapporteur on violence against women and girls, its causes and consequences, April 2023

Parental Alienation- Psychological Assessment

Mothers accused of parental alienation may typically find themselves ordered to have a psychological assessment, paying more fees to another parental alienation participant (this usually aims to find complex parenting relationship between mother and child causing the alienation, that alienation being suggested to lead to psychological abuse of the child)- effectively aiming to prove the mother is a danger to her children. Attempts have also been made to have Parental Alienation included in the World Health Organisation (WHO) classifications, unsuccessfully.

Is Parental Alienation – a health related condition?

The World Health Organisation (WHO) is an organisation that is looked to for global information on health, illness and diseases. It was founded in 1948 as a United Nations agency that connects nations, partners and people to promote health, keep the world safe and serve the vulnerable – so everyone, everywhere can attain the highest level of health.

World Health Organisation (WHO) had also considered whether parental alienation should be a recognised as an illness or disease within their International Classifications (specifically -11)[68].

According to WHO- the purpose of ICD-11 is:

'... to provide an internationally standardized classification for health diagnoses, to count health events and episodes of contact with healthcare for statistical purposes. Chapter 24 'Factors influencing health status or contact with health services' allows for the recording of circumstances or problems which influence an individual person's health status, but which are not in themselves an illness or injury. This includes the category 'caregiver-child relationship problem'.

'During the development of ICD-11, a decision was made not to include the concept and terminology of 'parental alienation' in the classification, because it is not a health care term. The term is rather used in legal contexts, generally in the context of custody disputes in divorce or other partnership dissolution.

'The broader category of 'caregiver-child relationship problem' was seen as adequately covering aspects of this phenomenon that could be the focus of health services.

'More recently, proposals to include the terms 'parental alienation' and 'parental estrangement' as index terms for 'caregiver-child relationship problem' were submitted and initially approved.

Following online commentary, the WHO-FIC Medical and Scientific Advisory Committee recommended clarification that inclusion of a term for search purposes does not signify endorsement by WHO of the term or its use. Following that clarification, comments and questions have persisted about the misuse of the term to undermine the credibility of one parent alleging abuse as a reason for contact refusal and even to criminalize their behaviour.'

11. UN Report- Custody, violence against women and violence against children Report of the Special Rapporteur on violence against women and girls, its causes and consequences, April 2023[69]

UN Special Rapporteur published a report on violence against women and girls, its causes and consequences which was submitted to the Human Rights Council pursuant to resolution 50/7. The report looked at the link between custody cases, violence against women and violence against children, with a focus on the abuse of the term "parental alienation" and similar pseudo-concepts.

> '... concern about the pattern of ignoring intimate partner violence against women in determining child custody cases across jurisdictions. Since raising specific concerns to Brazil and Spain, the Special Rapporteur has received reports of cases from countries where such violence has been ignored and where mothers making such allegations have been penalized by law enforcement and/or the judiciary responsible for determining custody cases. The tendency to dismiss the history of domestic violence and abuse in custody cases extends to cases where mothers and/or children themselves have brought forward credible allegations of physical or sexual abuse. In several countries, family courts have tended to judge such allegations as deliberate efforts by mothers to manipulate their children

and to separate them from their fathers. This supposed effort by a parent alleging abuse is often termed "parental alienation".

The report further examined ways in which family courts in different regions refer to "parental alienation" or similar pseudo-concepts in custody cases, ignoring histories of domestic violence, which may lead to the double victimization of victims of such violence.

The report went on to note that involving parental alienation is an extension of domestic abuse:

'Given the prevalence of domestic violence in intimate relationships, separation from a perpetrator can also be a highly dangerous period for the victim. Allegations of domestic violence tend to receive insufficient scrutiny by courts and to trigger problematic assumptions, for example that it causes little harm to the mother or child and that it ceases with separation. The consequences of domestic violence and its effects on children are also misunderstood and underestimated by judges, who tend to prioritize and grant contact with fathers. In doing so, judges fail in their duty to protect children from harm, giving abusive fathers unsupervised access to their children, including in cases where judges have found that physical and/or sexual violence has occurred. Where judges acknowledge the occurrence of domestic violence, they may regard it as historic, assuming that is in the past.'

Research and submissions received demonstrate that perpetrators of domestic violence can also misuse family law proceedings to continue to perpetrate violence against their victims, resulting in secondary traumatization. In this context, parental alienation may be employed as a useful tactic.'

12. Survival Checklist

My Survival Checklist

Women in abusive relationships are often gripped by fear and unable to leave and I certainly remember seeking advice, double checking and then triple checking before I finally found the strength to divorce. There are so many emotions, mostly fear; fear that if you start your step to escape and do not make it or fail in that process your life will be made ten times harder by the person that abused you...

'When we start you need to ensure I get my divorce, he will not let me live in peace if we don't make it....' were my words to the divorce lawyer as I finally leapt out of my marriage into the unknown. I had no checklist, no guidance, and alone so I lay out below some things that helped me survive and gave me glimmers of hope:

<table>
<tr><td>Finances</td><td>1. Find ways to save money.

2. Talk to Citizens Advice Bureau and any women's organisation that often offer free support for any general assistance.

3. If you have a bank account – especially a joint bank account – speak to the compliance officer at the bank, and confirm that confidentiality and data protection duties are in place (preferably in writing) by the bank before you discuss your options. Check if the bank is a member of the Financial Abuse Code. https://www.ukfinance.org.uk/system/files/2022-12/Financial-Abuse-Code-2021_Updated_2022.pdf

4. If you have never had a bank account and need to approach a bank to open one, check if the bank is part of any list of banks that are protecting against economic abuse. Ask for an officer that can help vulnerable customers, particularly if you don't have a copy of your passport or any previous records, but you want to open a bank account, and need help in completing Know Your Customer 'KYC' requirements.

5. If you have a joint account, ask the bank compliance officer to initiate a client refresh as your circumstances have changed.
Let them know that you need to be re-assessed under Customer Due Diligence and Client Classification requirements. Request information about banking services available to you individually. If there is any resistance, please ask the bank to consider their duties under the FCA AML and Client Classification obligations and FCA Consumer Duty See www.fca.gov.uk</td></tr>
</table>

Finances *(Continued)*	Remind the bank about confidentiality, that you are a vulnerable customer, and Consumer Duties should be applied to you. Ask for confirmation of what data protection and confidentiality provisions will be applied to you to ensure no information is shared with anyone else. If you think you may be subject to economic and/or financial abuse, refer to UK government economic abuse toolkit and Surviving Economic Abuse resources. **Ask if the bank has an ESG or Sustainability policy as it may contain commitments from the bank to help wider society.**
Devices	Check ALL your devices setting to ensure NO tracking is active, such as Find my iPhone is switched off, if unsure, take your devices to an IT company that can screen your devices or run a factory re-set to ensure there is no ability to track you.
Seek information on your options:	Seek information on your options: Search domestic abuse and official government websites such as: • Refuge • Women's Aid • Juno • UK Finance • NAGALRO • Social Work England • Ministry of Justice UK • Domestic Abuse Commissioner UK • Surviving Economic Abuse • Relate • REUNITE • Your local Embassy if you are based overseas • UK government websites (searching for Domestic Abuse, Economic Abuse, Financial Abuse, Coercive & Controlling behaviour)

Seek information on your options: *(continued)*	• Contact your local MP to understand what support they can give on domestic abuse issues *https://members.parliament.uk/FindYourMP* **Clear your internet search history *after!***
Preparing an Emergency Kit	1. Keep an emergency bag with clothes, toiletries and dry snacks for yourself and any children (include a toy). 2. If you can, purchase a cash passport card (available from money bureaus or the post office) and start saving money on it. 3. Keep a log of key numbers, passport numbers (if you can gain access to these documents), copies of bank accounts. 4. Keep the emergency kit somewhere safe with someone you can trust – or at work if this option is available to you.
Health checks	Keep up to date with health check. The stress may be impacting your health. Just because the abuse may not be visible on the outside, it may still be harming you on the inside.

This supplement is to empower and aide you.

Use the contents as you wish, and never give up hope.

"You survived the abuse. You're gonna survive the recovery."

Olivia Benson

Snakes and Ladders

My experience was *exactly* like a game of snakes and ladders!

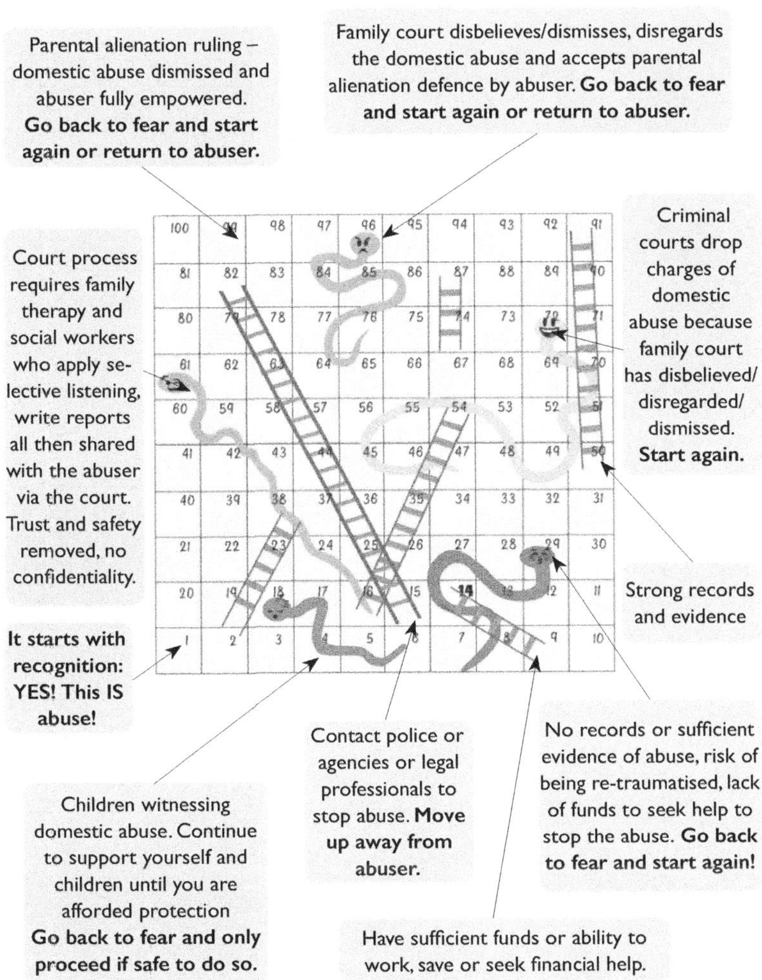

References

Quotes

1. https://assets.publishing.service.gov.uk/government/uploads/system/uploads/attachment_data/file/895173/assessing-risk-harm-children-parents-pl-childrens-cases-report_.pdf

2. https://assets.publishing.service.gov.uk/government/uploads/system/uploads/attachment_data/file/1158906/harm-panel-delivery-update.pdf

3. https://s3.documentcloud.org/documents/23813311/un-report-on-alienation-5-2023.pdf

Foreword

4. https://www.legislation.gov.uk/ukpga/2021/17/contents/enacted

5. https://www.gov.uk/government/news/new-guidance-will-ensure-all-forms-of-domestic-abuse-are-recognised

6. https://assets.publishing.service.gov.uk/government/uploads/system/uploads/attachment_data/file/895173/assessing-risk-harm-children-parents-pl-childrens-cases-report_.pdf

7. https://www.judiciary.uk/judgments/re-c-parental-alienation/

8. https://www.gov.uk/government/publications/the-family-court-and-domestic-abuse-achieving-cultural-change

9. https://caselaw.nationalarchives.gov.uk/ewhc/fam/2023/399

Warwickshire County Council v The Mother & Ors [2023] EWHC 399 (Fam)- Expert Trish Barry-Relph 'Reunification Plan was misguided and the role of Ms Barry-Relph unhelpful'

10. https://www.theguardian.com/law/2022/dec/07/uk-woman-whose-children-were-removed-against-their-wishes-loses-appeal

11. https://www.bbc.com/news/uk-66531409?s=09

12. https://assets.publishing.service.gov.uk/government/uploads/system/uploads/attachment_data/file/895173/assessing-risk-harm-children-parents-pl-childrens-cases-report_.pdf

Breaking the Cycle

13. https://www.gov.uk/government/publications/the-family-court-and-domestic-abuse-achieving-cultural-change

14. https://assets.publishing.service.gov.uk/government/uploads/system/uploads/attachment_data/file/895173/assessing-risk-harm-children-parents-pl-childrens-cases-report_.pdf

Chapter 19 The Teller

15. https://www.gov.uk/government/publications/public-sector-toolkits/economic-abuse-toolkit-html

Chapter 28 Gaining Some Financial Access

Note also this aligns to the economic abuse examples as set out in the UK Economic Abuse Toolkit-

16. https://www.gov.uk/government/publications/public-sector-toolkits/economic-abuse-toolkit-html

17. https://survivingeconomicabuse.org/what-is-economic-abuse

Chapter 31 The Appeal

18. https://survivingeconomicabuse.org/what-we-do/research-and-evidence/economic-abuse-a-global-perspective/

19. https://survivingeconomicabuse.org/wp-content/ uploads/2022/11/Understanding-economic-abuse.jpg

Chapter 39 September

20. Sarah J. Harsey & Jennifer J. Freyd (2022) Defamation and DARVO, Journal of Trauma & Dissociation, 23:5, 481-489

Chapter 40 Prove It

21. https://assets.publishing.service.gov.uk/government/uploads/system/uploads/attachment_data/file/895173/assessing-risk-harm-children-parents-pl-childrens-cases-report_.pdf

22. Assessing Risk of Harm to Children and Parents in Private Law Children Cases (Harm Report) UK Ministry of Justice, June 2020

https://assets.publishing.service.gov.uk/government/uploads/system/uploads/attachment_data/file/895173/assessing-risk-harm-children-parents-pl-childrens-cases-report_.pdf

23. Assessing Risk of Harm to Children and Parents in Private Law Children Cases – Implementation Plan: delivery update UK Ministry of Justice, May 2023

https://assets.publishing.service.gov.uk/government/uploads/system/uploads/attachment_data/file/1158906/harm-panel-delivery-update.pdf

24. https://www.womensaid.org.uk/family-courts-remain-an-unsafe-and-traumatic-place-for-women-and-children/

25. Too years, too long: Mapping action on the Harm Panel's findings (womensaid.org.uk)

26. https://www.womensaid.org.uk/wp-content/uploads/2022/06/Two-Years-Too-Long-2022.pdf

27. https://www.womensaid.org.uk/kvk-a-retreat-from-progress-in-the-family-courts/

28. https://www.womensaid.org.uk/womens-aid-responds-to-the-harm-panel-progress-report/

29. https://www.gov.uk/government/publications/the-family-court-and-domestic-abuse-achieving-cultural-change

30. https://www.theguardian.com/society/2023/jul/18/family-courts-domestic-abuse-commissioner-england-and-wales-children-at-risk

Chapter 42 The Decision

31. https://www.gov.uk/government/publications/the-family-court-and-domestic-abuse-achieving-cultural-change

32. https://s3.documentcloud.org/documents/23813311/un-report-on-alienation-5-2023.pdf

33. https://s3.documentcloud.org/documents/23813311/un-report-on-alienation-5-2023.pdf

DAC_Family-court-report_Methodology_2023_Digital-1.pdf (domesticabuse-commissioner.uk)

Assessing Risk of Harm to Children and Parents in Private Law Children Cases (publishing.service.gov.uk)

Chapter 44 Staying Strong

34. https://caselaw.nationalarchives.gov.uk/ewhc/fam/2023/399-

Supplement

Introduction

35. https://assets.publishing.service.gov.uk/government/uploads/system/uploads/attachment_data/file/1158906/harm-panel-delivery-update.pdf

36. https://assets.publishing.service.gov.uk/government/uploads/system/uploads/attachment_data/file/895173/assessing-risk-harm-children-parents-pl-childrens-cases-report_.pdf

37. https://assets.publishing.service.gov.uk/government/uploads/system/uploads/attachment_data/file/895173/assessing-risk-harm-children-parents-pl-childrens-cases-report_.pdf

38. https://sigbi.org/assets/Specialist-Domestic-Abuse-Courts-How-special-were-they-in-2022.pdf

Section1 Domestic Abuse

39. https://www.gov.uk/guidance/domestic-abuse-how-to-get-help

Section 2 Domestic Abuse Act 2021

40. https://www.legislation.gov.uk/ukpga/2021/17/section/1/enacted

Section3 Practice Direction

41. https://www.justice.gov.uk/courts/procedure-rules/family/

Section 4 Economic and Financial Abuse

42. https://www.legislation.gov.uk/ukpga/2021/17/section/1/enacted

43. https://www.gov.uk/government/publications/public-sector-toolkits/economic-abuse-toolkit-html

44. https://survivingeconomicabuse.org/wp-content/uploads/2022/11/Under-standing-economic-abuse.jpg

45. https://survivingeconomicabuse.org/news/sea-responds-to-announcement-on-new-child-maintenance-powers/

46. https://www.legislation.gov.uk/ukpga/2023/24/enacted

47. survivingeconomicabuse.org/wp-content/uploads/2023/09/ Seen-yet-sidelined_SEA_2023.pdf

Section 5 Assessing Risk

48. https://assets.publishing.service.gov.uk/government/uploads/system/uploads/*attachment_data/file/895173/assessing-risk-harm-children-parents-pl-childrens-cases-report_.pdf*

Section 6 Assessing Risk

49. https://assets.publishing.service.gov.uk/government/uploads/system/uploads/attachment_data/file/1158906/harm-panel-delivery-update.pdf

50. https://assets.publishing.service.gov.uk/government/uploads/system/uploads/attachment_data/file/895173/assessing-risk-harm-children-parents-pl-childrens-cases-report_.pdf

Section 7 Social Work England

51. https://www.socialworkengland.org.uk/

52. https://www.socialworkengland.org.uk/standards/

Section 8 Preparing For Court

53. https://assets.publishing.service.gov.uk/government/uploads/system/uploads/attachment_data/file/1158906/harm-panel-delivery-update.pdf

Section 9 Child Proceedings

54. https://www.socialworkengland.org.uk/standards/

55. https://www.judiciary.uk/judgments/re-c-parental-alienation/

56. https://www.gov.uk/government/publications/the-family-court-and-domestic-abuse-achieving-cultural-change

Section 10 Parental Alienation

57. https://s3.documentcloud.org/documents/23813311/un-report-on-alienation-5-2023.pdf

58. https://s3.documentcloud.org/documents/23813311/un-report-on-alienation-5-2023.pdf

59. https://www.who.int/standards/classifications/frequently-asked-questions/parental-alienation

60. https://www.gov.uk/government/publications/the-family-court-and-domestic-abuse-achieving-cultural-change

61. https://s3.documentcloud.org/documents/23813311/un-report-on-alienation-5-2023.pdf

62. https://www.cafcass.gov.uk/2021/01/14/cafcass-reissues-position-on-parental-alienation/

63. https://www.judiciary.uk/judgments/re-c-parental-alienation/

Recommendation 10- Domestic Abuse Commissioners Second Report-

64. https://www.gov.uk/government/publications/the-family-court-and-domestic-abuse-achieving-cultural-change

Assessing Risk of Harm to Children and Parents in Private Law Children Cases Implementation Plan: delivery update - UK Ministry of Justice, May 2023

65. https://assets.publishing.service.gov.uk/government/uploads/system/uploads/*attachment_data/file/1158906/harm-panel-delivery-update.pdf*

66. https://s3.documentcloud.org/documents/23813311/un-report-on-alienation-5-2023.pdf

67. https://www.who.int/

68. https://www.who.int/standards/classifications/frequently-asked-questions/parental-alienation

Section 11 UN Report Custody

69. https://s3.documentcloud.org/documents/23813311/un-report-on-alienation-5-2023.pdf

Section 12 Survival Checklist

70. ttps://www.ukfinance.org.uk/system/files/2022-12/Financial-Abuse-Code-2021_Updated_2022.pdf

71. www.fca.gov.uk

72. https://members.parliament.uk/FindYourMP

Other

73. https://www.gov.uk/government/publications/the-family-court-and-domestic-abuse-achieving-cultural-change

Printed in Great Britain
by Amazon

28810425R00138